The Deep-Rooted Marriage

COMPANION GUIDE

The Deep-Rooted Marriage

Cultivating Intimacy, Healing, and Delight

Dan B. Allender, PhD
AND Steve Call, PhD

W PUBLISHING GROUP

AN IMPRINT OF THOMAS NELSON

Published in Nashville, Tennessee, by W Publishing, an imprint of Thomas Nelson.

Published in association with Yates & Yates, www.yates2.com.

Thomas Nelson titles may be purchased in bulk for educational, business, fundraising, or sales promotional use. For information, please email SpecialMarkets@ThomasNelson.com.

Unless otherwise noted, Scripture quotations are taken from The Holy Bible, New International Version®, NIV®. Copyright © 1973, 1978, 1984, 2011 by Biblica, Inc.® Used by permission of Zondervan. All rights reserved worldwide. www.zondervan.com. The "NIV" and "New International Version" are trademarks registered in the United States Patent and Trademark Office by Biblica, Inc.®

Scripture quotations marked ESV are taken from the ESV® Bible (The Holy Bible, English Standard Version®). Copyright © 2001 by Crossway, a publishing ministry of Good News Publishers. Used by permission. All rights reserved.

Scripture quotations marked MSG are taken from *THE MESSAGE*. Copyright © 1993, 2002, 2018 by Eugene H. Peterson. Used by permission of NavPress. All rights reserved. Represented by Tyndale House Publishers, Inc.

Scripture quotations marked NLT are taken from the Holy Bible, New Living Translation. © 1996, 2004, 2015 by Tyndale House Foundation. Used by permission of Tyndale House Publishers, Inc., Carol Stream, Illinois 60188. All rights reserved.

Scripture quotations marked TPT are taken from The Passion Translation®. Copyright © 2017, 2018, 2020 by Passion & Fire Ministries, Inc. Used by permission. All rights reserved. ThePassionTranslation.com.

Any internet addresses, phone numbers, or company or product information printed in this book are offered as a resource and are not intended in any way to be or to imply an endorsement by Thomas Nelson, nor does Thomas Nelson vouch for the existence, content, or services of these sites, phone numbers, companies, or products beyond the life of this book.

ISBN 978-1-4003-4468-0 (ePub)
ISBN 978-1-4003-4460-4 (TP)

Printed in the United States of America
24 25 26 27 28 LBC 5 4 3 2 1

Contents

CONTENTS

Introduction

Most marriages, even good ones, rarely venture beyond the safety of shallow waters and smooth shores. It takes a rare and remarkable courage to set sail into an uncertain sea where most fear to venture. If you picked up this guidebook, then you are choosing to leave the placid harbor of complacency behind in order to discover the depths of intimacy possible when you navigate the brokenness and beauty of your marriage.

The risk in stretching out to the unknown requires learning how to hold both desire and disappointment. No one longs for what marriage is meant to be without suffering some unmet expectations. The journey we are inviting you to travel will at times feel bumpy and uncertain, but our goal is as certain as the Spirit who lives in you and promises to complete the good work that was birthed in you.

No matter how challenging the process, you will know more of the fullness of God and more of the fullness of what it means to love well and be loved as you were intended to know. Our sincerest hope is for you to grow into the person who can daily love your spouse as the "face of God." This is a far bigger dream than merely wishing for you both to have less conflict, or better sex, or more empathy for one another's heartache. It certainly includes the possibility of all those changes and more—but they are fruit and not the roots of how you relate in your marriage.

One reason many couples don't experience a deep-rooted marriage is the exhaustion of relentless busyness. We live in an era where a free half hour that is not filled with work, kids, chores, email, scheduling, commuting, exercising, church, friends, or an occasional night out is rare. If you are in a good marriage, to want more when so many demands pull at you both may seem indulgent.

If you are in an okay marriage, one that lacks vitality and joy but is good enough to get by and stave off divorce, the same issues of exhaustion and busyness are at play. But the risk to take on what is not well in your marriage worries you—because the cure might be worse than the disease you've learned to live with. While it is easy just to keep going and hope things will get better, expecting new outcomes by repeating old patterns is the definition of insanity.

Perhaps you are in a wilting, dying marriage and your partner is reluctant or hostile to communicating openly and honestly, reading a book, engaging with a companion guide, or seeing a therapist. Your situation may feel hopeless, but your courage to pick up this guide says otherwise. As difficult as it may seem to believe, your willingness to address the exercises and questions here, even alone, will change the tenor and direction of your marriage. It may not transform your relationship the way you wish, but it will unquestionably alter how you engage your heart and your spouse.

How your partner responds to such changes is uncertain, but what is clear, and what we can say with confidence, is your spouse will become better or worse. He or she will not remain the same. No one can remain the same when exposed to courageous, compassionate love. This companion guide can help you love your spouse far more than you may imagine possible, although the outcome ultimately remains beyond your control.

Objectives

Our hope is that this guide provides information, insight, and inspiration as you pursue three main objectives:

1. Grow in your awareness of embedded patterns as you plow up hardened soil.

If you want to grow good fruit, the ground needs to be plowed and furrowed. Good seed grows best in soil that is soft, pliable, and ready to receive rain, sun, and nourishment from the decay of past patterns. This plowing requires looking at both the present ways you and your spouse relate in several key areas and then pondering how those patterns developed from the past. Our focus will move from what drew you together—what we have called your origin story—to how you relate today.

Once your origin story and your operating patterns, both problematic and life-giving, are clearer, you will move into a second phase:

2. Disrupt embedded patterns as you assess the soil and fertilize with new insights and fresh compassion.

No soil, or soul, or marriage is perfect. We all need to grow, and growth requires change. For most, change involves disruption and some degree of discomfort—experiencing the pain we frequently work to avoid. Such relational soil analysis requires breaking the surface and exposing what lies beneath, knowing the soil must be enriched if roots are to grow deep and produce good fruit.

Or consider how the apostle Paul spoke about growth in the simple metaphor of taking off one set of clothes and putting on another that is more fitting for what you desire. In order to grow, you need to take off patterns that are now problematic, even if those patterns were once a means of survival in difficult days of the past. This process will help you both name and become aware of how the past is playing out in the present. Until you can understand, grieve, and let go of why you do what you do, you are less apt to develop new patterns.

The final growth phase replaces your old default response patterns with new practices that can bring good fruit to your marriage because your roots are healthy and strong.

3. Create new patterns and practices that nourish the roots and produce good fruit.

God has promised that we are new creatures who have the capacity to be reconciled to one another and to create new worlds and relationships that are rich in honor and delight. We intend to help you engage conflict more wisely and kindly and resolve what cannot be resolved by a win/lose competition but can unite you in blessing by exploring and embracing your differences. A nearly infinite number of remarkable moments are ahead for you if your goal is to be the face of God for your spouse. Your focus is on how to move the present into a different future.

This guidebook is designed to help you maintain your focus and move closer to your goals for growth. As a companion to our book *The Deep-Rooted Marriage*, this guide will help you dig deeper and implement the practices essential for changing yourself and your marriage. Drawing on key points in the book, you will find this guide useful in personalizing and applying what's required for growing deeper roots and better fruit. This companion guide does not replace the Bible, good care, community, or therapy. It is an ally, an adjunct to the work of the Spirit of God.

We are honored to be on this journey with you. Both Steve and Lisa join Becky and me

(Dan) in sharing what we have witnessed, discovered, experienced, and observed, certainly as professional therapists but more significantly as broken individuals committed to loving our partners. We have been enriched, as individuals and as couples, by practicing what we preach and seeing marriage therapists for our respective relationships.

Our journeys as couples don't indicate specific problems to be solved as much as they reflect our no-holds-barred, passionate commitments to become whom we are meant to be as individuals and as a husband or wife. There are matters we would have likely not engaged without the kind, wise, generous disruption of good friends and therapists opening our eyes to truths we didn't have the strength or courage to engage on our own.

While this guide cannot take the place of a trained marriage therapist, it can help clarify where you are, how you got here, why you got here, where you want to go, and how to move forward. In the six sections ahead, you will discover two crucial questions designed to help you experience growth in this process. Each question draws on content and examples from the book as well as supplemental videos featuring the four of us—Dan and Becky, Steve and Lisa—discussing our experiences.

Questions and exercises accompany each key question followed by a third section, Nourishing the Roots, which distills that section's key principles into action points. While the big questions in each section can help facilitate discussion with others should you choose to complete this guide in a group, Nourishing the Roots is intended for your personal exploration and reflection, which you are free to share—with your spouse, your therapist or trusted confidant, or group members—as you choose.

To make the most of your journey with this guide, please consider the personal investments necessary for your transformation: *time*, *perseverance*, and *risk*. Engaging with the content here will not require countless hours to experience growth. The key is the quality of your *time* spent engaging with the material, not necessarily the quantity of time invested. You will be asked to remember, reflect, and write, and it is better to build on small increments than attempt to devote hours of effort that only leave you exhausted. Be faithful in the small, and you will see results that amaze you.

Perseverance is also essential. We encourage you to consider a commitment of three months for engaging this material. This allows roughly two weeks per session, which provides ample time for considering the content in the midst of breaks and busyness. If you are on this journey with a group, then you can discuss this pace and what works best, allowing adequate time between each meeting for individual processing and reflecting. Depending on your spouse's level of engagement, you will also want to include time for sharing your responses and discussing the material contextually in your relationship.

Finally, you must be willing to *risk*. Time and consistency are crucial, but if you don't count the cost, you will likely find other endeavors more satisfying. The truth is dangerous and disruptive, calling us out of the comfort and lethargy of a distracted life. You will be breaking ground on unaddressed or poorly addressed heartache from the past and the present. You will likely experience, to some degree, present trauma as you engage past trauma.

We will guide you through those moments, but it requires you to risk trusting that the process will lead to growth, to goodness and wholeness. You will need to take risks—individually and relationally. Foremost, you will need to take new risks with your spouse. No one fully and completely trusts his or her spouse with every intimate thought and emotion, but you must take risks if you desire more than you're presently experiencing together. In addition to relating to your spouse, perhaps the greatest risk is to see whether God is true to his word. Growth is as much a theological process as it is psychological.

You might also consider risking vulnerability by doing this work with other individuals and couples. Something profoundly healing can be experienced in letting our lives be held and known and suffered by others. We each need authentic community to grow as people and perhaps even more so as couples.

Whether you engage with this guide in a group or not, it will help to have others willing to support you. Keep in mind, though, that receiving their perspective and input about what they see in your marriage can be illuminating as well as disturbing. Within each section, particularly Nourishing the Roots, you will find guidance for both giving and receiving support from other group members and trusted individuals.

No matter how enriching or challenging your marriage may seem, most couples began with hope-fueled infatuation and pleasure-filled delight in each other. Of course, there were issues, but love would win the day, and your rough edges would be smoothed over in due season. You may have been naïve and emotionally reckless, surfing the dopamine and oxytocin highs in your brains, but something drew you two together.

You need to remember this connection, especially when you're struggling. You must hold one another with awe and gratitude. This reverence is more than holy optimism or positive thinking. It is the willingness to ask, *How did God attract two remarkably different human beings into marriage?* It is the courage to believe, *Our roots can grow deeper and our relationship can flourish in ways that we can't even imagine right now.*

Dig deeper with us in the video series using the QR code at the back of the book.

Daring to dream with you,

Dan

Part 1

Starting Where You Are

It is impossible to get an Uber or Lyft if you don't know where you are or where you're going. These apps require you to enter an address for pickup as well as a specific destination. Drivers want a clear sense of where they will find you and where you want to go.

The same is true for growing your marriage. Where are you? Where are you going if you continue in this direction? Is that where you and your spouse want your marriage to be? The willingness to consider these questions already puts your marriage countless miles ahead of most couples.

Even as you choose to move forward, the process of assessment is not without risk and complexity. In this section we want to guide you through a productive and honoring process to know where you are and begin considering how you got there and where you want to go.

Here are some big ideas we will explore in Part 1:

- Your marriage is an ongoing story with highs and lows, joys and heartache, a story that continues shaping you and your spouse, for better or worse.
- Without being honest about where you are in your marriage and getting confirmation from your spouse and trusted friends, you will likely remain complacent and resigned to what you have. You will rarely experience what is possible if you fail to engage what is true.
- Identifying and acknowledging where you are in your marriage allows you to look at the past and see the individual stories and dynamics intersecting in the present.
- No matter how difficult or sweet your marriage is, God created you for more than whatever you are experiencing today.
- Your marriage is where redemption is meant to grow. God intends for it to be not merely good or happy but transformative.

Dig deeper with us in the video series using the QR code at the back of the book.

1 . 1

Where Are You?

Every marriage is a story of two people formed by different worlds joining together to create a universe that has never existed before. Your marriage is unique in all its goodness and in all that needs redemption. In a state of unawareness, we'll continue making efforts, but not in ways that lead to change. "Just trying harder" will keep us stuck in ingrained patterns that cause disconnection, and eventually we will conclude that change is not possible.

THE DEEP-ROOTED MARRIAGE, P. XI

Most people don't reflect on where they are and where they want to go unless they're implementing a diet-and-exercise plan or a retirement savings program. Even with these endeavors, progress often remains elusive. Lasting change requires commitment, consistency, and sustainability. We don't like to face our deficits and struggles, nor do we want to take tangible steps to create a different future even if we don't like where we are in the present.

But there's great value in looking at where you are and gauging the distance from where you want to be. Areas of dissatisfaction or frustration in your marriage can help you see where you are and what's not working. Similarly, identifying what you enjoy most about being in relationship with your spouse also provides a barometer of present health and future potential. If you struggle to identify these basic extremes, this lack of awareness is still revealing.

Regardless of how you would describe your relational dynamic today, whether it is on the rocks, soars above the clouds, or lives somewhere in the middle orbit of reality, please remember: *you and your partner are meant for more.* No matter how challenging or intimate your marriage is, God created you for more than whatever you are experiencing right now.

You and your spouse are not merely in relationship to survive or even have a "good" marriage. Your marriage is meant to be a taste of heaven, a glimpse back into Eden, and an anticipation of what will one day be true. You are the face of God to each other.

- What one word comes to mind to express where you are in your marriage right now? Why this word?
- What is your hope or desire as you begin this process of growing deeper roots in your marriage?

Breaking the Surface

If you want a flourishing garden, you need to break up the ground's surface and assess the status of the soil. Breaking the surface allows the soil to aerate beyond the thin top layer. Depending on its composition, density, and balance of ingredients, the soil may require supplemental elements such as fertilizer or even manure.

After all, your goal is to tend the dirt in order to help nutrients reach the roots. From well-nourished roots, your flowers, shrubs, and trees will grow, producing stems and stalks, trunks and limbs, blossoms and fruit reaching skyward. Meanwhile, those well-fed roots continue to spread and burrow deeper underground.

Intrusive obstacles to growth must also be addressed. If you are dealing with weeds, it is not enough to cut them off at the top and hope they go away. You have to dig down deep into the soil to extract their roots and kill what will diminish your crop. It is messy, dirty work, but the result of good care and experienced wisdom is delicious, nourishing fruit.

Your marriage works the same way. This metaphor can easily become a cliché if you engage with it only as an optimal or idealized comparison. It's only when you begin seeing the intricacy of the comparison that you grasp the ongoing process of growth. When you dig down into your story, you will reach the cause of whatever you're seeing at the surface level now. When you learn to allow your spouse to reveal what's buried beneath the surface of his or her story, you will have new insight about how to care for him or her.

Let's consider another metaphor: Every marriage is a tapestry. The threads of a vertical life interlace with a horizontal life, forming a stunning picture on one side and rough knots on the other. Both people are beautiful because they were made in the image of God. They both are also broken and flawed due to their traumatic ancestry and natural proclivity to mishandle their pain. Each of them is a glorious mess as an individual and even more dramatic and compelling as a couple.

It is in this place of intimacy that both our imperfect and exquisite qualities are most visible. There's no one who knows more about your brokenness or has seen you shine at your best like your spouse. We all are meant for this—to know and be known—and it is in marriage that we can see into the kaleidoscope of our complex identities most clearly. The closest intimacy provides exclusive access to our deepest places.

As we open ourselves to our spouses, we also can open ourselves to the heart of God, allowing his extravagant grace, compassion, and delight to trickle down into the core of us. It is, in fact, part of why he brought us together, so we could know intimacy with each other and with him—and experience his love in profound and powerful ways.

As you begin assessing where you are with your marriage right now, if you and your spouse are willing, you will bring your past threads, both beautiful and stained, and together weave a glory that, if seen from the vantage point of eternity, reflects the incomprehensible beauty of God. While no one is perfect and no marriage is without flaws, every marriage can defy the past, redeem the present, and live for the future.

Including yours.

- What rises up within you as you consider where you are in your marriage currently? Check all that apply.

_____ hopeful	_____ depressed
_____ determined	_____ relieved
_____ anxious	_____ worried
_____ excited	_____ dreadful
_____ fearful	_____ ashamed
_____ eager	_____ angry

_____ curious	_____ cautious
_____ frustrated	_____ sad
_____ skeptical	_____ lonely
_____ uncertain	_____ resentful
_____ discouraged	_____ hurt
_____ connected	_____ confused
_____ disconnected	_____ other:

- As you review the responses you checked, which two or three seem the most significant? Why do these stand out? Write them below and consider the source of their provocative impact.
- What kind of relational, emotional, or therapeutic work have you and your spouse done up until now? What impact have these experiences had on your relationship?
- What has disappointed you about past efforts to grow or improve your marriage? What did these past efforts reveal about the condition of your relationship?
- What has surprised or delighted you about past efforts to work on your marriage? What did you learn about yourself and your spouse from these experiences?

Letting In the Light

Nearly all living organisms require light in order to grow and flourish. The impact of sunlight on aboveground plants and trees can be especially noticeable as most of these herbaceous systems grow toward the light source. You've likely seen flowers that bloomed at odd angles because of their location in proximity to sunlight or trees with branches reaching around an urban obstacle toward the sky.

As your guides throughout this process, we, Dan and Steve, don't presume to illuminate your understanding of marriage in totally new and radical ways. What we do hope to share in each of these sections is simply a fresh perspective, a new approach to aspects of your relationship with your spouse. At times the experiences we want to share and the observations we want to make may seem glaringly obvious, and other times we hope to shed light on the dynamics of your marriage that have remained a mystery until now.

Living Water

Your marriage is where redemption is meant to grow. You will become whom your marriage exposes and invites you to be. This is a far richer and more compelling vision of marriage than only getting along or resolving conflict through compromise or learning more effective communication skills. With this redemptive purpose of marriage in mind, you and your spouse are either becoming more like Jesus together and because of each other—or you are not.

If the mention of God, Jesus, or the Holy Spirit offends you or undermines our credibility because of your past faith-related experiences, please know that we understand. Many religious people have made marriage a fetish or, worse, an unequal bondage of rules and roles rather than what God invites us to: a wild faith journey into the hope of transformation. If you are not particularly religious or your personal faith is in transition, then take the risk to give us a shot, and see where it takes you.

In order for transformation to take place in your marriage, supernatural love is required. Just as adequate hydration is essential for your garden, the living water that Jesus described in conversation with the Samaritan woman at the well is necessary for your growth as individuals and as a couple. In order for your roots to grow and flourish, they must be saturated with grace, kindness, curiosity, and compassion that go beyond your human capacity.

It seems fitting, even ironic, that this woman had been trying to quench the deep thirst in her soul with relationship after relationship—but none of them satisfied for long. Only as Jesus accepted her and surprised her with the unexpected power of his love and mercy did this woman finally experience what her marriages never provided. Read their encounter below and then use the questions that follow to reflect on the essential ingredient of living water for your own growth.

So Jesus left the Judean countryside and went back to Galilee. To get there, he had to pass through Samaria. He came into Sychar, a Samaritan village that bordered the field Jacob had given his son Joseph. Jacob's well was still there. Jesus, worn out by the trip, sat down at the well. It was noon.

A woman, a Samaritan, came to draw water. Jesus said, "Would you give me a drink of water?" (His disciples had gone to the village to buy food for lunch.)

The Samaritan woman, taken aback, asked, "How come you, a Jew, are asking me, a Samaritan woman, for a drink?" (Jews in those days wouldn't be caught dead talking to Samaritans.)

Jesus answered, "If you knew the generosity of God and who I am, you would be asking *me* for a drink, and I would give you fresh, living water."

The woman said, "Sir, you don't even have a bucket to draw with, and this well is deep. So how are you going to get this 'living water'? Are you a better man than our ancestor Jacob, who dug this well and drank from it, he and his sons and livestock, and passed it down to us?"

Jesus said, "Everyone who drinks this water will get thirsty again and again. Anyone who drinks the water I give will never thirst—not ever. The water I give will be an artesian spring within, gushing fountains of endless life."

The woman said, "Sir, give me this water so I won't ever get thirsty, won't ever have to come back to this well again!"

He said, "Go call your husband and then come back."

"I have no husband," she said.

"That's nicely put: 'I have no husband.' You've had five husbands, and the man you're living with now isn't even your husband. You spoke the truth there, sure enough.

"It's who you are and the way you live that count before God. Your worship must engage your spirit in the pursuit of truth. That's the kind of people the Father is out looking for: those who are simply and honestly *themselves* before him in their worship. God is sheer being itself—Spirit. Those who worship him must do it out of their very being, their spirits, their true selves, in adoration."

JOHN 4:3–18; 23–24 MSG

- Do you agree that in order for your marriage to grow, Jesus is meant to be central in your life? Explain what intrigues you or makes you uncomfortable with this notion.
- What word or phrase in this passage stands out to you or resonates in a personal way? How is it significant for where you are right now?
- Why do you suppose the Samaritan woman was wary of Jesus? How did he surprise her with his questions and responses?
- Jesus was kind, respectful, and playful with this woman. How do those qualities show up or fail to be practiced in your marriage?

Sharing Fruit

Throughout your journey with this guidebook, you will hear from Dan and Steve, along with some input and discussion from their wives, Becky and Lisa. Via the video link below, we want to share some examples of our experiences, both as husbands and as therapists, and to walk you through an orchard of good fruit. Just as we wrote about in *The Deep-Rooted Marriage* book, we will share some of the good, bad, and ugly moments from our marriage experiences.

We don't presume our marriages are like yours necessarily or share them as a model for what to do; we offer them as examples of how marriages can look. We all are different, but most couples share some commonalities that reflect the tenacious process of growing strong roots and good fruit.

The four of us have not arrived or perfected our marriage relationships. But we have become more aware of tender areas to treat with care and of broken tendencies we can redirect. We have learned to address them collaboratively over the decades of our respective marriages, and we no longer feel caught in the relational patterns that emerged when we were younger. We are much more aware of when they creep in and have learned to gently steer out of them.

We've become quicker to speak compassion and grace when we stumble. To receive truth and gentleness when we feel vulnerable. To free and empower each other when we feel stuck. Divisive moments have become less frequent and are resolved more quickly, which has not only brought relief but left room for more joyful, fulfilling connection.

All told, little by little, we've allowed ourselves to be seen and known and reached by the other in increasingly deeper ways, generating a kind of goodness and sweet intimacy that leaves us in awe. We still have conflicts, hurts, tension; we are still human. But we are so much further along than we were. We are more in tune with ourselves and each other, with how God's love and life can reshape, reassure, and renew us. And, year after year, we are surprised by the ways God keeps letting us *taste the more* and *become the more* we are meant to be, together. This is the fruit of our wisdom, gleaned from an orchard of experience, that we want to share with you here.

1.2

How Did You Get Here?

*Understanding the past allows us to make sense of what's not working
in the present. If we don't explore our earlier stories, we won't grasp
how our histories of brokenness and beauty are playing out now.
And we'll be bound to repeat them in one form or another.*

THE DEEP-ROOTED MARRIAGE, P. XI

Superheroes have origin stories explaining how certain abilities and superpowers came to exist. Typically, the hero experienced extreme pain or duress in ways that resulted in the discovery of extraordinary power, strength, and endurance. Romantic comedies have meet-cute moments in which the prospective protagonists have a memorable, quirky, fiery, or funny first meeting. They are often at odds even as they sense attraction. As you begin assessing where you are now in your marriage, you will borrow a little bit of both narrative genres to help you see how you got to this point.

Over a series of countless events in your childhood, you developed relational patterns that enabled you to survive whatever pain you continually encountered. As an adult, you instinctively live out those same patterns in the present. If you want a redeemed future and a more beautiful marriage, excavate and sift through what shaped you and your spouse in the past.

For most of us, this will feel either too dangerous or unproductive. The familiar present patterns may seem more tolerable than uncovering past wounds and stirring up old memories.

What good does it do to look back at what's already been done? You can't change the past, right? Why mess with what you'd rather forget when there are real and urgent issues present in your marriage that need addressing? Because the past reveals how the roots of your marriage were formed—and how they can grow deeper and healthier.

- If a filmmaker created a romantic comedy about the way you and your spouse came together, what would it be called? Why?
- What unsettles you the most when you consider looking at past moments in your story? What superpowers did you form to survive all that you've been through?

Breaking the Surface

Patterns that are unhealthy in a marriage are often related to past relational heartache and trauma—whether acknowledged or not. For change to occur and new growth to begin, it is imperative to plow up those patterns and understand their rooted past and purpose. We will be asking you to consider more deeply your family of origin and key stories that have shaped your way of being in the world.

It is one thing to understand how patterns were developed in the past, but it is essential to make the connection of how you live out your past traumatic survival patterns in the context of threat and hurt in the here and now. Much of the time, the past patterns and current behaviors may not appear to have a cause-and-effect clarity. If you dig deeply enough, however, you will see how the roots from the past shape the direction of the tree in the present. There are ways for these root patterns not only to change but to bring even more tasty fruit than ever before.

Nearly all marriages begin with giddy pleasure, robust hope, and an ocean of naïveté. Research indicates the dating and courtship period floods our brains with sufficient oxytocin and dopamine comparable to doing cocaine for about nine months to a year. Once the honeymoon fades, the biochemicals and hormones that brought us such an overwhelming rush of love can't remain at that level, even if we demand they do so. Does that mean it is all an illusion? A big divine bait and switch?

While you may feel duped during an extended conflict or the exhaustion of caring for a sick child while your spouse travels for work, you must also appreciate the overwhelming high of those early days. We are given in the early days of our marriage a taste of Eden in the fresh, exhilarating newness of knowing and being known. The differences between us intrigued and excited us, perhaps with some tensions, but usually the ups and downs felt like part of a well-written drama that ends with a lovely conclusion.

Look a little more closely, though, and most couples had moments when there was conflict and testing. Courtship was not, for most, a simple, easy process, which may be why we enjoy the over-the-edge rom-coms because we know our courtship had moments like a roller-coaster ride with uncertainty about the conclusion. But love won in the end, and we went off to our honeymoon hoping for happily ever after.

There was innocence and goodness without being fully tested and tried in the crucible of a new career or going to school while working and developing friendships and eventually dealing with the big four: in-laws and children (family), money, sex, and deciding how to spend limited leisure time. Life events interrupt life, and the long marathon replaces the short sprint of courtship.

Remembering how you came together, however, is crucial to going forward. We seldom take time to walk through pictures, old letters, favorite songs, restaurants, and memories from our earliest years. We may still hold those memories with nostalgia, but seldom do we study our past for clues about what has transpired over the years.

If you desire a healthier, deep-rooted marriage, start walking through the remnants of the past. There are two reasons to do so: (1) Origin stories are full of clues about dreams and desires before disappointment erased innocence. We want you to bless desire and reawaken the dreams that brought you both together. (2) Your own personal meet-cute might also provide clues to course corrections that need to be made irrespective of how long you have been married.

Begin considering the past by creating a timeline, a visual chronology of how your relationship began and developed. For now, focus on the time from your first meeting to the first date, getting serious, talking about marriage, getting engaged, planning the wedding, the wedding and honeymoon, and the first three months. There may be other significant milestones and events that are unique to your origin story—be sure to add those as well. Here is a preliminary list of points to include on your timeline.

- First meeting
- First date

- First kiss
- Formally dating only each other
- First time the word *love* was used
- First conversations about marriage
- Engagement
- Wedding planning
- Wedding
- Honeymoon
- First living space

Once the timeline is relatively complete, then you can enhance it with photos, letters, keepsakes, and other memorabilia. If you have kept copious artifacts, videos, and pictures, then knock yourself out and start laying out the array on a large platform, like a dining room table. If you have only a few, don't be discouraged, but place what you have on a platform that you can keep up for an extended period without disturbance. You will come back to this later.

- As you consider your completed timeline, what stands out to you? What do you notice now that you may not have noticed before?
- Which moments are especially sweet and romantic as you look at the origin story for your marriage? Which moments make you cringe—with pain, dread, or judgment?

Letting In the Light

Every couple struggles, to some degree, with leaving the psychological and relational demands of their family of origin. As much as you and your spouse love each other, you each came into your marriage with certain loyalties, demands, duties, and patterns of behavior related to each of your parent(s) and sibling(s). You may not consider trauma to be a part of your upbringing, and perhaps it wasn't to some degree, or you may struggle to find seasons of your childhood that were not traumatic. Most couples are stunned to see what suddenly seems so obvious as you begin looking at how each of you learned to relate, connect, and handle conflict.

So many partners in marriage break one another's hearts without having the insight to understand why or the language to deal with it. You may not have considered that you married one another to escape the trauma of your families or that marrying each other did not necessarily enable you to escape the pain of past trauma within your families of origin. You may have married one another in an attempt to redeem what you had lost and suffered without naming what you had each lost and suffered—which means those deep hurts keep hurting. And they keep ruling and dividing your hearts in how you relate.

No matter how you view your marriage's origin story, please consider that what draws couples together can eventually divide them. What brought you and your spouse together was a hunger for redemption of the harm that you can barely see, let alone name, and that failure to name and acknowledge results in a framework for untold present and future suffering to play out.

Not engaging your stories is like cutting off the top of a weed instead of yanking it out by its roots. If you consider your marriage to be a tree that you hope will grow and flourish, those weed roots will keep crowding your tree roots until you do something about them. The weed roots you are being invited to address are the ways, means, and consequences of past heartache and trauma.

To go forward, you must first go back. Enter the fray of past heartache to have the capacity to dream and live out a radical new future. Become a student of your own story as well as your spouse's.

Living Water

Entering the past and connecting what you find there to present dynamics in your marriage may feel like a costly battle, one you're not even sure you can win right now. The further back you go, the more likely it is that you will discover only more profound losses, heartaches, and harms both you and your spouse endured. You may already be tempted to give up and settle back into the comfort of what's familiar. To prevent giving up or losing sight of how the past can inform the present and change the future, you need an ebenezer.

In the Bible, when a great act of God occurred, an ebenezer would be built. Usually, an ebenezer was a grouping of stones, like a cairn, that signaled to those who passed by that they were on holy ground. Translated from the Hebrew as "stone of help," an ebenezer signifies that something is worth remembering, that this site serves as both monument and memorial. In the passage below, you can see how Samuel raised up an ebenezer after defeating the Philistines.

While Samuel was sacrificing the burnt offering, the Philistines drew near to engage Israel in battle. But that day the LORD thundered with loud thunder against the Philistines and threw them into such a panic that they were routed before the Israelites. The men of Israel rushed out of Mizpah and pursued the Philistines, slaughtering them along the way to a point below Beth Kar.

Then Samuel took a stone and set it up between Mizpah and Shen. He named it Ebenezer, saying, "Thus far the LORD has helped us."

So the Philistines were subdued and they stopped invading Israel's territory. Throughout Samuel's lifetime, the hand of the LORD was against the Philistines. The towns from Ekron to Gath that the Philistines had captured from Israel were restored to Israel, and Israel delivered the neighboring territory from the hands of the Philistines. And there was peace between Israel and the Amorites.

Samuel continued as Israel's leader all the days of his life. From year to year he went on a circuit from Bethel to Gilgal to Mizpah, judging Israel in all those places. But he always went back to Ramah, where his home was, and there he also held court for Israel. And he built an altar there to the LORD.

1 SAMUEL 7:10–17

Notice that Samuel not only set his ebenezer between the places of Mizpah and Shen, but that he also built an altar to the Lord in Ramah, where he made his home. It seems reasonable to assume that Samuel liked having these tangible reminders of God's involvement in his own life and in the lives of the people of Israel.

As you continue exploring and excavating your origin story, an ebenezer can do the same for you. It can be both anchor and lighthouse, both beacon and bastion. Raising an ebenezer is not a form of denial or pretense that harm has not occurred. It is not a nice bow, wrapping up a package that was barely opened. An ebenezer is a rite of honor that acknowledges

- someone bigger than you brought you and your spouse together;
- something deeper in the two of you pursued and risked safety to become one;
- something was captured by the other that needs to be named and honored no matter the quality of your marriage today.

As you come to realize there is a divine purpose in bringing you together and holy desire was part of what captured you by the other, then it is time to build your own ebenezer, your own cairn. So go get some rocks—seriously. Yes, it may feel silly or stupid, but just go with it.

Depending on where you live and your living arrangements, you might use large rocks to create a formation in your garden. If you're in an urban apartment or tighter quarters, then you might go with some small, smooth river stones on a patio table or indoor shelf. It doesn't matter the size and shape and location as much as simply choosing to set an ebenezer for your marriage.

As we continue guiding you through the process of deepening your roots, we want you to remember that blood and death and loss have brought you and your spouse together. A Creator made the stones and brought you together, and the battle ahead can be faced because the battle behind you is already victorious.

Wherever you place your ebenezer, we hope it is large enough (given your space) and sufficiently prominent so you can daily see the monument to the past and the promise for the future. Yes, they are just stones. Just as your marriage is a relationship. But your relationship is vastly more than a legally certified entity.

As you go through the remainder of this companion guide, you might find that a stone needs to be added. It might be a bigger stone on the bottom that represents a restoration of the foundation. It might be a smaller stone on the top that represents the growing fruit that is sweet to the taste.

Tend to your ebenezer, and your memory will tend to your future—because there is more to be done regarding your past and how it shapes the present.

Sharing Fruit

Any good fruit produced in your marriage will be the result of building awareness by looking back, understanding your hurts and tendencies, and seeing what needs tending to. So even as we share a bit more about our own individual stories and how they perfectly collided in our marriage, you are encouraged to continue looking back.

Begin with the family dynamic in your upbringing. What were you accustomed to? What was your role? Identify the behaviors you repeated in response to people around you and how you coped with fears or unmet needs. See if you can spot ways you continually felt hurt or frustrated and what longings developed as a result.

Next, think back to when you met your spouse. Maybe it was at school or church, at a bar or a wedding, through online dating or an awkward blind date. No matter where you met, there was a magnetic energy that both propelled you toward each other and created tension between you. There are those who knew after a single minute, *This is the one.* Others knew in the first few minutes, *I'd rather be skinned alive than be with you*, but somehow, against all odds or reason or sensibility, they married.

Ask the question *How did you meet?* in light of what drew you to each other. You met scores of people you might have married, but you didn't. Usually, it boils down to something physical, relational, and spiritual.

"We just clicked."

Or "We were at loggerheads from the beginning, but something still felt right."

Or "I don't know other than it just felt inevitable."

What is truly inevitable is "What I need fits what I think you can provide, and thus, I will demand it from you"—and, again, this is all unconscious. The fit is far deeper than what most of us have considered.

1 . 3

Nourishing the Roots

Marriage is a wild, at times terrifying, journey into the fullness of what love, with honesty and humility, can bring to this earth. Your marriage is meant to transform, redeem, and free you to be fully alive.

THE DEEP-ROOTED MARRIAGE, P. 11

You are now invited to further explore the current status of your marriage, where you are and how you got there, by doing a more personal exercise. This third section of each part will vary from the usual format of the other two. This section is intended to provide a more hands-on approach to the work you're doing, creating space for more intimate work than the previous two sections.

Also, if you are completing this guidebook as part of a group, Nourishing the Roots is intended for you to complete on your own along with your spouse, if they are willing to participate. The focus is on growing together as you think about the health of your marriage and what needs attention moving forward. These exercises are designed to increase awareness of your stories and relational patterns as well as draw you closer together.

For this first Nourishing the Roots exercise, you're going to complete a more thorough assessment of your marriage and use it as a tool to begin an ongoing conversation with your spouse. Think of it as a deeper and more accurate picture of the health of your marriage. While you have already checked vital signs in the prior two sections, now it is time to get more specialized as you, along with your partner, focus on your relationship. Consider this as more of a full blood panel analysis than just taking your temperature, more of an EKG than a quick listen with the stethoscope.

This process will involve responding to twenty statements and giving a score between 1–5 for each, based on how well or how poorly you think you and your spouse are doing. You are each encouraged to complete this assessment on your own before coming together to compare and discuss. Here are the score values:

5: Superb
4: Very Good
3: Satisfied
2: Struggling
1: Failing

Superb—Scoring a 5 implies a high probability, even if not perfect, that the statement holds true for you and your partner most of the time. When you respond with a 5 to the statement, it usually reflects that your spouse is your favorite person to be with because you share a love of learning and a consistent openness to good care, honesty, and honor.

Very Good—Scoring a 4 suggests your response is affirmative and steady but perhaps not as consistent as reflected by a 5. If you score a statement with a 4, then it's likely that you're often at ease with one another's company and enjoy being together but don't prioritize personal growth and marital growth as much as getting along and enjoying life.

Satisfied—Scoring a 3 states that you and your spouse might affirm the summary statement about 50 percent of the time. You likely experience as many disappointing times as times when you feel joyfully connected. If you respond with a 3, you and your partner might be busy, stressed, and chronically exhausted, typically avoiding conflict or areas that could cause distress. Contempt and avoidance are more present than in a thriving marriage, but you get along most of the time while likely finding more pleasure in other activities (children, work, hobbies, sports, friends) than in your marriage.

Struggling—If you choose a 2, then it implies there is more frustration and disappointment in this area than not, even if things go well enough occasionally. Scoring a statement with a 2 acknowledges that you're struggling and poised for either major transformation or further division and isolation. There is likely a high prevalence of contempt, fault-finding, blame-shifting, and periods of isolation. This is a traumatized marriage even if one or both of you deny it. There is always hope, but the process ahead is best done with a well-trained marriage counselor.

Wilting—If you respond with a 1, you're acknowledging major ruptures, past and present, where there have been significant betrayal and unresolved heartache. Your marriage may seem to be teetering on the brink of dissolution, but thankfully there is still an ember of hope. If there has been a threat of physical or emotional harm in your relationship, it is wise not to proceed with completing the companion guide without the care and protection of a good therapist and a small group of confidants who can guide you through the slow rebuilding of trust and care.

Those are your scores and valuations, and here are the three parts to the process of this assessment. First, respond to each statement with a number between 1 and 5 that best reflects your relationship with your spouse at present.

1. We can be in conflict and keep the process safe and productive. _____
2. I feel like he/she is interested in my thoughts and listens well. _____
3. When contempt arises, we can name it and return to kindness after some time apart. _____
4. We each have some clarity on how our past influences our way of engaging the other. _____
5. We can engage differences in desire or thought with curiosity. _____
6. We can talk about difficult issues with sufficient care and honor to make progress. _____
7. We enjoy one another's company. _____
8. My spouse thinks about ways to honor and serve me that feel life-giving. _____
9. My spouse knows what triggers her/him and can address what's happening without blaming me. _____
10. I know how to care for my spouse when she/he hits a low point. _____
11. My spouse receives my comfort and forgiveness when he/she fails. _____
12. When I feel lonely, his/her presence feels comforting. _____
13. We can approach scary issues slowly and over time without rushing to a quick solution. _____
14. My spouse can address the influence of his/her family of origin in our marriage. _____

15. My spouse is not possessive or jealous of my time with others. _____
16. My spouse gets me even when I don't understand what is going on with me. _____
17. We know how to return to one another when there has been a rupture. _____
18. We laugh a lot together. _____
19. We know how to carve out time for each other in a busy schedule. _____
20. We share household tasks in a way that enhances our relationship. _____

Next, after you have responded to all the statements, look over them again and consider why you gave the score you gave. Then, beneath each statement, write a sentence or two summarizing the basis for why you scored it with that number. If a specific situation comes up in your mind as to why you gave that score, then write a few words to describe what occurred.

Finally, the third task in this process of assessment is by far the most challenging: Have an honest, engaged conversation. Compare your numbers with those of your spouse. Where there is a disparity—one gives a remark a 5 and the other, a 3 or lower—highlight that comment. Where there is a disparity of a single number, the difference may be important, but it is also highly subjective to the way we read or interpret a question. Once all the disparities have been highlighted, read to each other what you wrote beneath that statement and begin a conversation.

Follow these guidelines as you converse:

- **Refrain from debating or trying to change the other's mind or score.** Instead, ask two to three questions (no more) for the sake of clarification. If your spouse uses a recent or past event to illustrate, this is not the time to give your side of what happened or to blame your spouse for using that experience as an example.
- **Listen to the issues, themes, and desires that are prominent for you both.** As an example, an issue might be that you regularly avoid conflict. A theme in that instance might mean one person finally gets activated after repeated avoidance and says something harsh and the other apologizes and then it is dropped. A desire expressed in that context would be for both of you to develop a capacity to enter difficult conversations without the fear of making a problem worse.

Embrace: patience. No one can work on everything at once. It is wise to avoid addressing everything that will emerge from comparing your assessments. Use this as a picture that you can return to and study in more depth in the weeks to come.

Embrace: present engagement. Once a couple begins to talk about past hurt and conflict, there is a tendency to want to "story-tell" past failures, which is normal yet unproductive for learning what you're both sharing about your marriage. Try to avoid past scripts and summaries. Don't get sidetracked and lose engagement with one another.

Avoid: defensiveness. The moment defensiveness arises, it is best if one or both of you stops and names it. It is likely defensiveness will arise to protect oneself from current hurt related to past failures. Listen to the tone, language, and intention of defensiveness and make sure you don't give that weed water or soil to grow.

Avoid: explanations. There is always a perceived reason you did what you did. Most of us often feel that if we can explain our motive or perception, the other will get why we did what we did. This is just a slightly more sophisticated form of defensiveness. It can look like a flower initially, but it is a weed.

Avoid: justifications. A justification is often a slightly hidden accusation that your spouse failed to understand what you were doing. It is an explanation with the energy of contempt. You are pleading your case while also taking the role of judge and jury and making your spouse the defendant.

Embrace: awareness. Every couple has a dark dance that causes conflict to spiral into greater harm. One person raises his or her voice, the other shuts down. When one shuts down, the more obviously angry spouse escalates and talks more. The quiet spouse plays with his/her ring and glances out the window or at their phone. The fight escalates and one or both throw up their hands and retreat into separate corners. Do not allow this assessment to become a weapon against one another. Use it as a tool for clarity and for aligning shared goals. Here are three goals you're encouraged to share as a result of this exercise:

1. Can we agree on two or three issues that need care and growth?
2. Can we acknowledge how certain patterns seem to keep us from offering good care to the other and to ourselves?
3. Can we commit to addressing everything and anything that keeps us from having an even better marriage?

If so, then you both know where you are and have some idea of where you want to go.

Part 2

Desiring More in Your Marriage

Your marriage is probably not defined by near-constant joy and perfect attunement to one another. No one's union reflects divine bliss all the time. Even as strong as your relationship may be, you are both sometimes aware that you hoped for more than what you've experienced so far. Perhaps more and more frequently, you endure long stretches with little to no delight or the intimate sense of connection you crave. Joy and deep satisfaction remain elusive, leaving each of you wondering what's missing or what you should be doing differently.

You may even have days when you try to deny the desire for deeper soul connection with your spouse, resigning yourself instead to a good-as-it-gets mindset. Conflicts and challenges likely compound what's not working, reinforcing the stagnation of the status quo. Regardless of how you describe your marriage right now, the good news, as we will explore in this second part, is that dissatisfaction reflects your desire for more—more trust, more joy, more connection, more intimacy.

Here are some big ideas we will explore in Part 2:

- Four areas of challenge and dissatisfaction can help reveal what's missing in your marriage and what you long for most: lack of delight, loneliness, contempt, and feeling stuck.
- Delight fades when you focus on control and preservation, settling for simply surviving when you could be enjoying so much more. Unresolved trauma steals delight and makes it feel unreachable.
- Loneliness results from lack of connection, attention, intention, and attunement. You are created to know and be known, to experience full heart engagement with your spouse. Loneliness is recognizing the absence of this connection.
- Contempt sets out to control another's behavior through shaming and belittling, often resulting in areas of conflict to avoid at all costs. It risks justification and isolation.
- Feeling stuck results from ongoing disappointment about whether it's possible to break free from the trauma-informed dynamics limiting and impeding intimacy in your relationship.

2.1

What's Working in Your Marriage?

*When our bodies feel a familiar old pain, our default response
will be to live out the past in the present, to do what we've always
done to self-protect. But, instead, we can learn how to consciously
disrupt the pattern and create a new story in the present.*

THE DEEP-ROOTED MARRIAGE, P. 130

Marriage offers the prospect of intimacy at a deeper level than any other human relationship. When you and your spouse met, grew to love each other, and chose one another in marriage, you likely experienced a connection that you expected to mature into an even richer bond of knowing and loving one another. Life together, however, is rarely, if ever, as Edenic as you longed for in those early days of coming together.

Sometimes instead of growing closer together, you intertwine until you hit an impasse. Or perhaps you feel like parallel individuals rather than a united couple. Regardless, the roots of your marriage can only grow so far when you encounter rocky soil, stunting your growth. In all likelihood, relentless life events—children, careers, illness or injury, relocation, elder care—have added stress to compound the challenges inherent whenever any two people live together with expectations of intimacy.

Over time unexpected patterns and powerful dynamics emerge. At your worst, you each find ways to harm one another in ways neither of you could have imagined on your wedding day.

At your best, you each surprise the other with moments of being known, accepted, and loved as expressed by words, actions, attitude, and touch. Chances are good that, most days, you're somewhere in between, wondering where your relationship is headed even as you long for more than what you're experiencing.

Depending on the duration of your relationship and your shared experiences, you may have resigned yourself to those longings remaining unrequited. Or you may enjoy the luxury of trusting that you both are committed to doing the hard work it takes to grow your deep-rooted marriage together. Either way, your dissatisfaction can be a healthy motivator as you begin to look more closely at what's working in your relationship and what requires attention—the unaddressed trauma you're each carrying—in order to grow closer.

- How would you sum up your expectations when you chose to marry your spouse? What helped shape these expectations?
- What's one of the circumstantial stressors that has contributed to where you are in your marriage right now?

Breaking the Surface

Take a deep breath and think back to when you met your spouse. Reflect on where you were in your life, what was going on in your family of origin, who your friends were, where you were living, and what you were doing with your education or career as well as your discretionary time. How did you and your spouse first encounter one another? Maybe it was at school or church, at a bar or a wedding, or through an online app or introduction from mutual friends.

No matter how and where you met, some kind of dynamic energy compelled you toward each other and created a certain magnetic tension between you. Perhaps you experienced intrigue and curiosity or formed an unfavorable first impression, but whatever occurred between you gained momentum—perhaps with some stops and starts along the way—that led to your commitment of marriage.

Whether you immediately surprised yourself by thinking, *This is who I'm going to marry*, or heard an internal red-flag warning of *Danger Ahead—Proceed with Caution*, some spark between you ignited some kind of connection. Perhaps your relationship led to marriage against all odds or seemed naturally inevitable to you both. Nevertheless, out of all the people you might have married, your spouse is the one you chose.

Why you made that decision may seem like a mystery now, or you may have gained clarity since then about what drew the two of you together. It often comes down to what we usually call chemistry, something visceral, physical, relational, emotional, and spiritual. Despite whatever misgivings or concerns either of you recognized, you agreed to move forward as a couple committed to one another, presumably for the rest of your lives.

What has likely become clearer over time is the underlying layers of your union. Consciously or subliminally, you each had a sense that the other had what you needed, could provide something you didn't have on your own or something no one else had fulfilled adequately thus far. With this covert assumption converted to conviction, you believed you were entitled to what your spouse could provide that would fill your needs, which leaves you frustrated and resentful, perhaps even bitter, when you experience anything less.

These unmet needs within each of you, and the likely unspoken expectations of fulfillment, must be identified and acknowledged. Before you do so, however, consider recognizing and celebrating the unique, strange, lovely, and often surprising ways that God brought you and your spouse into one another's gravitational pull. Your relationship was never an accident. And it is far more than merely a by-product of your cooperation within God's will. Your desire for more in your marriage reflects your felt need for restoration, your longing for the other to replenish what you sense you lack.

- How would you describe the first few interactions with the person who became your spouse? What appealed, intrigued, and attracted you to him or her? What caused you concern or made you pause?
- What did you initially see or feel or hope for in your spouse that had the potential to make you feel joy, contentment, and safety in your relationship?
- What was lacking in your family of origin, or was experienced only fleetingly or inconsistently, that you hoped you could find in your relationship with your spouse?
- What was one of the qualities or aspects of your spouse that you quickly found compelling and enjoyable? When did you first delight in your spouse?
- In what ways was your spouse similar to the kind of person you had imagined yourself marrying? How was your spouse different from the kind of person you had imagined marrying?

Letting In the Light

If you desire more for your marriage, then just imagine what your more might look like. How might God weave more beauty into your marriage, create something new in your hearts, bring a bit of heaven into your dynamic? What if some of what you longed for when you first married is still possible?

This may sound like such a bold, unimaginable possibility that it feels easier to leave it unasked. But even if it feels like an audacious ask, allow yourself just to explore and imagine what God is capable of doing in each of your hearts as he closes the distance between you. What would this kind of intimacy look like, feel like, and mean for your marriage?

Consider that God could guide you into healthier relational patterns, ones that foster love and truth, not division and resentment. He might help you each feel more known and delighted in, held up and believed in, supported and encouraged even at your lowest points. Perhaps conflicts that once seemed insurmountable could become bridges that facilitate clarity, openness, and movement over prior obstacles—something you can both understand and navigate together.

If such a notion seems too good to be true, so be it—but don't allow your skeptical idealism or fearful pessimism prevent you from dreaming about what could very well be within reach. Continue reflecting on how you met and came to marry your spouse, and then see if you can identify what got you to where you are today. Now imagine a new trajectory, one that's radically different and distinct from the cycle where you two currently expend a great deal of time and energy.

Living Water

You will recall that God intends for your marriage to transform you, not necessarily make you happy and completely fulfilled. Your spouse experiences the best and worst parts of you along with everything in between—just as you experience your spouse's highs, lows, and middles as well. But you each bring elements to your relationship that enrich one another and make you more as an interdependent couple than just the sum of your individuality. There is a kind of wholeness in your relationship that likely reflects God's original intention for your union.

We see a glimpse of such perfect intimacy in the story of creation recounted in Genesis. God, the great Creator, produced a world teeming with life in all its forms—plant, animal, fish, and fowl—to populate the earth, sea, and sky. His creation remained incomplete, however, until he fashioned human beings to reflect and contain his divine essence: "God created human beings; he created them godlike, reflecting God's nature. He created them male and female" (Genesis 1:26–28 MSG).

More details of God's process in creating humanity emerge in Genesis 2: "God formed Man out of dirt from the ground and blew into his nostrils the breath of life. The Man came alive—a living soul!" (Genesis 2:5–7 MSG). God placed the man within the garden created in the eastern part of Eden and instructed him to "work the ground and keep it in order" (Genesis 2:15 MSG). Still, something—or rather someone—was missing.

GOD said, "It's not good for the Man to be alone; I'll make him a helper, a companion." So GOD formed from the dirt of the ground all the animals of the field and all the birds of the air. He brought them to the Man to see what he would name them. Whatever the Man called each living creature, that was its name. The Man named the cattle, named the birds of the air, named the wild animals; but he didn't find a suitable companion.

GOD put the Man into a deep sleep. As he slept he removed one of his ribs and replaced it with flesh. GOD then used the rib that he had taken from the Man to make Woman and presented her to the Man.

The Man said,

"Finally! Bone of my bone,

flesh of my flesh!

Name her Woman

for she was made from Man."

Therefore a man leaves his father and mother and embraces his wife. They become one flesh.

The two of them, the Man and his Wife, were naked, but they felt no shame.

GENESIS 2:18–25 MSG

Over the centuries this passage has often been misinterpreted and misused to support cultural gender roles and patriarchal oppression of women. It has been used to create division and oppression and to shame individuals and couples, which is ironic considering its emphasis on naked vulnerability and union without shame. As challenging as it may be to put aside this passage's baggage for a moment, this origin story nonetheless depicts the relationship between man and woman as inherently intimate. It reveals something about our human need for togetherness and our desire for intimacy without shame.

Notice that woman was not created as an afterthought for man—she was made to complete God's divinely imbued human creation. Man and woman were formed from the same essence, bone of bone and flesh of flesh, in order to become one. This reference depicts not merely two bodies conjoined, such as in lovemaking, but parts coming together to complete the wholeness of humanity God created them to form. They are not only one flesh but naked without shame.

Read the biblical passage above once more, and then use the following questions to think through your observations and relevant implications.

- What is your initial reaction as you read this passage? What have you been told or taught about it previously? How do those associations impact your perspective now?
- How is the way you met and married your spouse similar to the way this man and woman first came together? And what's vastly different?
- What do you find problematic or troubling in this passage? Why? What's the connection between your concern and where you are in your marriage?
- How would you describe God's role in bringing the man and woman together? What motivated him to create them for one another?

Sharing Fruit

Every marriage is as unique as the individuals committed to one another. You may look back at the origin story of your relationship and see how similar you two were at the time, how easily you came together. Perhaps you shared a quirky sense of humor that no one else had ever gotten. You may have discovered that you shared similar family dynamics, ethnic heritages, socioeconomic statuses, or lifestyle values in the homes in which you grew up. Your personalities might have seemed like mirror images of one another, allowing you to see yourself in another person for the first time.

While there may have been some things in common, you may have been more drawn to one another by your differences. The quiet, reserved person appropriated vicarious excitement from the bold, gregarious extrovert. One may have been more logical and rational in his approach to life while the other followed her heart and its shifting tide of emotions. One more practical and resourceful, the other more decadent and creative.

Chances are good that you came together because of both your similarities and differences—and how they fit together. You shared enough of what you each valued in a relationship to risk exploring what was distinctly unfamiliar. As you continue thinking through what brought you and your spouse together, as you reflect on what remains dynamic about your relationship, you can now consider going deeper. Not to judge or exonerate, not to shame or blame, but to untangle and understand the separate threads of your stories that formed a joint strand when you married.

Throughout this process, allow curiosity to be your guide. As you consider your own story, look with a fresh perspective of compassion and acceptance toward yourself and what you have experienced. Use the same sense of curiosity, compassion, and acceptance in looking at your spouse's story and all he or she has endured. Even as you see the two stories coming together in your marriage, consider how the impact of each remains embedded in you as individuals—and comes out in the ways you relate.

2.2

What Would You Like to See
Change in Your Marriage?

*We can walk the path of healing, know deep connectedness, even
experience transformation—if only we will address our trauma
with brave honesty and consistent care. There is pain, yes; but
there is also hope for beauty, meaning, and joy. We have the option
of inviting the kingdom of God into our deepest places.*

THE DEEP-ROOTED MARRIAGE, P. 44

Comedians have a long tradition of drawing material from their marriage relationships. Whether shared in a stand-up monologue, sitcom, or improv ensemble, comic performers know the imperfections in our interactions with our spouses are rife with humor. The kindest depictions reveal joint ownership, emphasize the absurdity of human nature in general, and remind us to laugh as a way of celebrating connection. The cruelest variations, on the other hand, rely on dehumanizing, shaming, blaming, mocking, and justifying. Ultimately, there's nothing funny about disguising contempt as humor.

If you think for a moment, you can probably come up with good examples from both ends of the marriage-humor spectrum. Better still, you can likely recall moments when you and your spouse have done the same—used humor to break the tension and draw you together or used it as a weapon to belittle, humiliate, and separate. The approach to what you want to see change in your marriage often follows suit.

While it may be tempting to compile a list of your spouse's flaws and failures, you likely know that the way forward requires focusing on your own list. The temptation to point out the speck in your partner's eye rather than address the plank in your own will probably persist. But the way for both of you to see more clearly with the eyes of your hearts involves looking at how your individual stories collided into the shared narrative of the present. Simply put, identifying what you would like to see changed in your marriage relies on your willingness to first look within.

- How would you describe your spouse's sense of humor? How would your spouse describe yours? What do you both find funny?
- In your marriage, are the two of you more likely to use humor to connect or to divide? What recent example comes to mind to reinforce your answer?

Breaking the Surface

If you have identified where you are in your marriage and engaged in an honest assessment, then you have created space for your roots to grow deeper. As you begin reflecting on your origin story as well as your spouse's, you will discover some familiar terrain as well as some unexplored wilderness. Your trek through this landscape of the past will not leave you wandering in circles to ruminate on regrets or wistfully wonder, *What if?* Instead, you will focus on detecting how your past shapes your present.

In other words, the way forward requires looking behind. You may have heard, "The past is never dead. It's not even past" from William Faulkner's *Requiem for a Nun*. This statement implies that we can plumb the past endlessly, and we will never fully finish all it offers or resolve all it reveals. You will, however, gain needed insight as you proceed together to address the questions we invite you to consider. Keep in mind, though, that new and vital insights will arise again and again in the future regarding the role of the past.

Once you become a detective to the dynamics of your marriage, you will see certain situations distinctively differently, gaining perspective on why you each do and say certain things in particular situations. Nonetheless, the mystery will never be fully revealed. You are shaped by your family of origin and ancestors in ways that cannot be fully understood no matter how thoroughly you mine the past.

You will likely never know the extent of your culture, ethnicity, neighborhood, education, past trauma, and what appear to be random acts of violation and beneficence that have changed the direction of your life. But, in the face of mystery, some clear dynamics have influenced your way of being in the world that must be named, understood, and transformed.

Facing your past requires vulnerability, time, and safety. You may fear that you will discover realities that make interacting with your parents, siblings, and others more challenging. You may have been told that facing what is true about one's parents is disloyal and violates the fifth commandment of honoring our parents. At a deeper level, if you name what is true, you likely fear the more significant loss of what you still long to receive: blessing. It is easier to say, "I am not into blaming my parents" than to face their inevitable failures and still forgive and love. This is the wilderness you are invited to explore and navigate.

The journey, no matter how painful, is ultimately worth the cost. Conflict has likely occurred in your marriage due to issues related to your parents and in-laws. A familiar battleground in most marriages emerges out of your tendency to defend or justify something said or done by your parents, discounting your spouse's irritation. This raw and tender terrain may have a lot of scar material built around the wounds. Be aware of where you feel compelled to defend, justify, or explain. To say "My parents did the best they could" is both defensive and untrue. It is a way of saying they don't have the capacity to change in the past or present, which is a lie.

To name what is true—both broken and beautiful—requires safety. Imagine if you have covered over your father's brusque and, at times, demeaning anger, and your spouse has angrily prodded you to face it. To own it now brings the fear that your spouse will pile on and use your past reluctance against you. For you to do this work and invite your spouse to do and share his or her own requires safety, honor, and respect.

Past hurt and current fear, often bound up in shame, are a given—and openly addressing them helps you develop the skills of creating safety for each other.

- How often have you looked to your childhood, upbringing, and family of origin for clues about how you relate in your marriage? What rises up in you when you consider looking for such connections?
- What concerns, fears, and apprehensions do you hold as you consider exploring your past

in order to understand your present? If you allow yourself to catastrophize, what's the worst outcome lurking in your imagination?

- How willing is your spouse to look at his or her origin story in order to understand the present patterns you share in your marriage? What's required for you to take ownership of your story regardless of how your spouse addresses his or hers?

- Think for a moment about times when you have said, either to yourself, your spouse, or someone else, "My parents did the best they could." What's required in order to give yourself permission to hold them accountable for what is true without blaming them or victimizing yourself?

- How can you hold the tension of identifying and acknowledging the truth of the past while choosing to love and forgive those who contributed to your wounds?

Letting In the Light

In order for your roots to grow deeper and healthier, you need safe space.

Creating the safe space of fertile ground is easier said than done. One of the hardest things to do when you feel unsafe is name it. Many people would rather ignore the warning signals (suppress, deny, numb) or try to override them (distract, escape, consume addictive pleasure). You may not even realize how your body responds when you feel unsafe. As you become more aware of what's going on, you may notice your gut tighten, your hands clench, or your tone of voice become flat. There are countless somatic indications that you are feeling stress from a lack of safety.

When you feel a change in your body, try to tune in and name it. Here are some strategies to consider: Tune in to yourself from head to toe. Close your eyes and count to ten and imagine releasing the stress throughout your body with each count. Take a deep breath and hold it for three or four seconds before exhaling for double the number of seconds you held. You can also take a drink of water and feel the liquid cooling your mouth as you swallow. Go outside for fresh air. Wash your hands in warm water. Try different practices that help you become aware of your body and facilitate relaxation.

If you are in a discussion or interaction with your spouse, notice what is happening in them. How do you read their body language? What expression do you see? How are they holding or carrying themselves?

Ask for input: "I feel defensive right now, and my shoulders feel tight. Can we pause and let me work through what is going on?" Similarly, you might be aware of their stress more than your own and invite them to pause with you and take a moment before resuming. A pause is the first step to regaining ground when you begin to fragment and feel overwhelmed or feel like shutting down, extremes that therapists call hyperarousal (you feel agitated or edgy, you need to move, to express your big feelings, to find relief of some kind externally) and hypoarousal (you feel lethargic, tired, foggy, you want to detach and rest or sleep, retreat within yourself for relief).

As you learn to recognize stress in your body and a sense of unsafety, consider the context. What triggered or contributed to your change in stress level? What did your spouse say or do or look like that loosed something within you? What did you say or do or look like that caused something to rise up in your spouse?

We often experience a change in our stress level before our brains can make sense of what is happening. We often don't know what is causing the rise in cortisol. Our bodies and brains need time to ponder the change. If we feel pressure to be productive and transparent, to figure things out immediately, then we will not let the truth come to us in small doses, which is usually how it emerges.

So pause. Relax. Listen.

It is in these moments that our bodies crave containment and comfort. Ask your partner for their perspective. If there is some clarity, then put it into words: "I feel like you are waiting for me to go further with this discussion than I am ready for." Once a context can be addressed, even if there is more, a plan can be made to restore safety.

State your intention to ground your partner.

When we don't feel safe, we begin to fragment—our thinking and capacity for reasoning goes, to some degree, offline. We need to find solid ground. The last thing we need is someone, including ourselves, judging us for what we feel. Resist the tendency to label what you're experiencing, and instead, let yourself be curious and patient.

You also need the affirmation from your partner: "I can see you feel disrupted and perhaps unsafe, and I want to provide whatever safety will ground you. What do you need from me?" The invitation is often enough to reestablish safety. Sometimes there will need to be a break to take a walk or pray. Whatever is required in order to restore safety is always far more important than the immediate conversation, which is ongoing.

Living Water

Inviting God into your examination of the past acknowledges that some issues and wounds are bigger than you or your spouse can handle alone. Such an invitation requires humility. It reflects your willingness to hope in what you cannot yet see or perhaps even imagine but dare to believe can happen.

While instantaneous miracles of healing for you and your spouse are possible, most lasting change happens as you do the hard work, day by day and week by week, of intentional collaboration—with one another and with the divine. Daring to hope and trust the power of the God who looks like Jesus necessitates faith in what may not seem logical, rational, realistic, or feasible according to human abilities and limitations.

You can desire more in your marriage for the rest of your life without experiencing the transformation and growth available to you. When you bring faith into the process, however, you increase the likelihood of eliminating barriers and facilitating fruition. We frequently see the impact of faith—even the tiniest mustard seed of wanting to believe—in the healing encounters between various people and Jesus as recorded in the Gospels. One in particular stands out for the question Jesus asked of someone in need:

> Soon another Feast came around and Jesus was back in Jerusalem. Near the Sheep Gate in Jerusalem there was a pool, in Hebrew called *Bethesda*, with five alcoves. Hundreds of sick people—blind, crippled, paralyzed—were in these alcoves. One man had been an invalid there for thirty-eight years. When Jesus saw him stretched out by the pool and knew how long he had been there, he said, "Do you want to get well?"
>
> The sick man said, "Sir, when the water is stirred, I don't have anybody to put me in the pool. By the time I get there, somebody else is already in."
>
> Jesus said, "Get up, take your bedroll, start walking." The man was healed on the spot. He picked up his bedroll and walked off.
>
> JOHN 5:1–9 MSG

In light of the situational context here, the question posed by Jesus demands our attention—just as surely as it must have compelled the man to reconsider why he was there and what he truly wanted. This man had been an invalid for almost four decades. Hanging out near the five alcoves of this pool, known for its angelically inspired healing qualities, this man likely despised the cruel irony: he could never enter the waters quickly enough to experience healing because of the ailment so desperately needing a cure.

Jesus had just returned to Jerusalem and was apparently headed to the temple when he saw this man lying near the Sheep Gate close to the well-known pool known as Bethesda. He didn't introduce himself or make small talk—Jesus cut to the quick of the matter and asked, "Do you want to get well?" (John 5:6).

If anyone else had been audacious enough to ask such an obvious question, it would have come off as cruel, callous, or terribly inconsiderate. Yet Jesus, who didn't need to ask to know the answer, of course, gave this man a choice regarding what happened next. Keep in mind that crowds of people in need gathered there regularly, including the blind, lame, and paralyzed. Surely it would have been safe to assume that if this man was lying there, he longed to be well, that he would return even in the face of his humiliating slowness and lack of assistance. Why else would he have been there?

It's safe to assume Jesus was not being unkind, inconsiderate, or indifferent to the desire of this man's heart. Christ intentionally asked the most relevant question required for healing to take place—not for his own benefit but for the man poised for a miracle. The question is timeless and one you are invited to consider as you proceed to explore the past in order to facilitate healing in the present—and to change the course of your future with your spouse.

- What spiritual history, values, and practices do you and your spouse share? Over the course of your marriage, what role has faith played in how the two of you relate and make decisions?
- What aspects of your marriage would you like to see change but struggle to imagine happening? What hinders you from inviting the healing power of Jesus into these areas?
- Why do you suppose Jesus asked this man, obviously an invalid, if he wanted to be well? What does the man's response to Jesus reveal about the man's desire for healing?
- Jesus knew if he healed this man on the spot, everything in the man's life would change. When you consider the real possibility that the changes you long to see in your marriage are possible, even likely, what feelings are stirred?

After reflecting on your responses to these questions, consider spending a few minutes in silence before God, opening your heart to the possibilities of change now being planted.

Sharing Fruit

Triggers are our natural response—physically, mentally, emotionally—to unaddressed harm. Similar to the way a military veteran might hit the ground when hearing a car backfire, you might defensively duck from what your spouse directs toward you—or deflect it and retaliate. Triggers take you back to situations that, at some level, have dynamics in common, even if they're not immediately apparent.

For example, imagine being in the middle of a conflict with your spouse when you suddenly feel cold and brittle with all your walls of defense going up. Perhaps the threat of being humiliated by your spouse hearkens back to when you were mocked by your father for vulnerably expressing your fears or when your mother belittled you for expressing sadness. You may have witnessed in your spouse as well a seeming overreaction to something rather benign that you said or did.

Every human being gets triggered in the present by harm done in the past. Our body harbors the threat and natural defense response from our past and by default wants to use the same strategy when we perceive a similar threat now. This tendency is written in our body and will make us vulnerable to misperceiving and mishandling situations that provoke stronger responses than seem appropriate.

As I (Dan) have shared in *The Deep-Rooted Marriage*, I have often felt tension with Becky when I engaged her space in the kitchen. For example, the other night I was about to use olive oil for a stir-fry when Becky interjected, "Don't use olive oil with a strong flame."

Immediately a nastiness began rising in me, and I wanted to say, "Well, then you finish the meal!"—making sure my contempt punctuated my hurt. Simply put, I was triggered by her remark that she offered in an attempt to be helpful. I felt belittled, shamed because I didn't know better, incompetent in her domain.

My anger and the nasty reply that lingered in me felt utterly justified, but due to our work together, I was far quicker internally to name my trigger. As a result, I quickly owned my reactive response, which was not hidden from my beloved. Aware of how I became conditioned to defend myself when feeling patronized or humiliated by my mother, I owned my reaction and knew it for what it was—my own issue and not intentional harm from my wife's words.

Triggers are never to be blamed on our spouses, yet we are tempted to do so. Even if our spouses have failed us, triggers are not used to justify the harm we have endured. Owning a trigger doesn't make us the problem or at fault. It is simply the acknowledgment that deep in our soul we are experiencing a trauma response and need to pause and tend to what's going on inside before proceeding to engage with our spouses.

In naming that I was triggered, I assured my wife that I would not overreact or blame her, but it might take me a few moments to get saffron oil instead, restart the stir-fry, and return to myself. Triggers are not meant to be resolved but engaged. Our vulnerable parts need more care and engagement through understanding their origins and functions. Your work on your family of origin sets the foundation for that work, which in turn helps you begin identifying other traumas that continue to linger and get triggered.

2.3

Nourishing the Roots

Sensing a threat affects every part of our being—our bodies, brains, hearts, and spirits. Its impact is comprehensive and complex, changing our ability to relate to ourselves, others, and God. It is a shock to our system, one we are wired to react to instantaneously in biological, psychological, and relational ways: we fragment, we numb, and we isolate.

THE DEEP-ROOTED MARRIAGE, P. 77

As you will recall, this third section invites you to a more hands-on and personal approach as you apply what you're learning and exploring at a deeper level. Also, as a reminder, if you're completing this guidebook as part of a group, Nourishing the Roots is intended for you to complete on your own along with your spouse, if he or she is willing to participate. You're welcome to share your experience doing these exercises with your group at the next meeting, but the primary purpose is to continue increasing story-awareness, seeing relational patterns, and identifying triggers between you and your spouse.

Root-Nourishing Exercise

This root-nourishing exercise allows you to enter your story and begin excavating insights about what you have carried with you into the present. We will guide you through four scenarios that will enable you to reflect on the world that was your earliest learning classroom. As you imagine and enter each scene, try to notice the details from your own similar experiences when growing up. You might find it helpful to write a little story in order to describe the reality of the actual memory evoked.

If the scene seems especially emotionally charged, try writing it in third person (referring to yourself as "he" or "she") as if you are watching it onscreen. As uncomfortable or challenging as it may be to write about, getting words down can help make the experience more concrete. You will have future opportunities to elaborate and fine-tune some of the particularities. And you will also have the chance to share what you write with your partner and read whatever he or she wants to share with you.

As you write each scene, ask yourself: What age was I? What big time markers (grade at school, birth of a sibling, moving to new home, etc.) provide context? What did I look like at that age? (Do you have any photos of yourself at that age?)

When you reflect on the scene, recollect the place where the scene occurred. If you have a photo of the room or place, look at how the stage was set up. If there are no photos, can you draw a schema of the room—where was the bed, the chairs, the table? What could you see from your bedroom window? Where did you spend the most time when at home?

The goal here is to get you closer to what you felt and experienced then, as a child, not only what you feel and think today. At first, attempting to enter the felt experience of an eight-year-old boy or ten-year-old girl might seem impossible, but your brain has the capacity, with a bit of practice, to feel a portion of what occurred. As you enter and explore each scenario, note what seems to come to the surface within you as well as what you experience in your body.

Scene One:

You are eating dinner with your family, and tension begins to build. It might be a typical family dinner on any given weeknight when you were growing up. Perhaps it's a big meal with extended family for a holiday or special occasion, such as someone's birthday. Only this time the tension escalates, and conflict ensues and intensifies.

What has caused this problem? What happens next? Who speaks first? How do your mother and father (if both are present) engage one another in the conflict? If the conflict is about you, then what is your response? If the tension and conflict involve a sibling or other family member, what is your role in the scene? How does the conflict end? What do the others at the table do as the tension builds and then comes to an end?

What do you notice about your role once you have entered this scene? Or if you struggled to recall a specific scene of your own, what did you feel trying to imagine this? What did you do to mitigate the conflict? How did you soothe the tension in your body after the conflict?

Scene Two:

You bring home your report card with grades that your parents or caregivers find unacceptable. You didn't perform up to the standard of what is your best. You anticipate fallout as you wait on your parents to see your grade for each area of study and then react or respond.

What happens? What is said, and what is the tone of the exchange? Who speaks? If both parents were present, what is each's involvement in the interaction? What consequences result from the conversation?

If you struggle to imagine this report-card scenario, imagine that you tried out for a sports team, the school orchestra, or a performance in a play. What happens when you don't make the team, achieve the first chair, or get the lead part? What is the response? How does the primary parent respond to you?

Scene Three:

You have experienced something at school or in the neighborhood that has made you sad. It might be a close friend moving away, the death of a grandparent or loved one, or a teacher suddenly being replaced. You are unable to hide what you feel, and there is sadness, anger, or withdrawal that noticeably reveals something hurtful has happened.

Is your emotional expression noticed? Who responds to your hurt? What is the response—what is said, and what is the tone? What are you expected to do because of the interaction? If there are two parents in your home, are there differences in the way one parent responds to your sadness compared to the other? Is there tension between your parents if they are both present?

Consider how you felt with each parent's response. Did you feel closer to one parent than the other? Did one parent seem to favor you differently than the other? If it seems natural to proceed, then consider how you were treated differently than your siblings. And please note: no parent treats all the children in the family the same. Whether due to birth order or favoritism, to circumstances or context, each child is uniquely engaged by both parents.

We will address and explore the category of triangulation in more detail in Part 3. For now, though, know that it is common for one child to be favored over the other(s), much as Joseph in the book of Genesis was his father's favorite. This deadly dynamic can be raw and profoundly tender to address.

If a parent chooses you, then likely there was some conflict and envy experienced by your other parent. Undoubtedly, there was envy and animosity from your siblings if you had them. It can be extremely difficult to admit you were chosen. It is also excruciating to admit you were not the favorite. But you were either chosen, or you were not. Most families prefer to pretend that all the children were treated the same—a thin veneer unable to support the glaring truth beneath such a claim.

Scene Four:

Consider a time when one parent's favor of you or a sibling played out in some demonstrative, tangible way. Perhaps you were either given more power and privilege than your siblings, or you witnessed one of your siblings being chosen over you. There was clear inequality, though, in how you were treated based on your status.

Which parent did you feel closest to as you were growing up? How did that parent favor you? Who was chosen as more worthy of delight and honor than you? What did it feel like to be with a parent who didn't choose you? How did that parent's envy play out against you? How did your sibling's envy play out against you, or how did your envy play out against the chosen one?

Processing Your Experiences

Every family creates stress and trauma for children due to parental failures. It is a universal reality. The quality of your attachment style reveals how these sometimes subtle (as well as not so subtle) experiences coalesce into long-term, multilayered issues.

Secure attachment to your parents or primary caregivers is experienced through attunement, containment, and the ability to repair rupture. Consider each of these by answering the following questions.

Attunement: Were your feelings recognized and addressed with kindness and care? If not, were you blamed or ignored? The lack of attunement makes it difficult to trust ourselves and what our body feels and more challenging to trust others with our thoughts and feelings.

Containment: Were your responses to experiences of harm, conflict, and trauma in your home given space to be addressed with honor and respect? If you were feeling dysregulated and angry, was it safe to be angry without fear of reprisal? If you were in tears, was it safe to feel hurt, or were you shamed or ignored? If you withdrew, did anyone notice and seek the cause of your withdrawal? Containment gives ground for dysregulation to be engaged with strength and compassion. Lack of it leaves you drawing your own conclusions about how to survive and endure pain, tension, and trauma.

Repair of Rupture: Did your parents apologize when they failed you? Did they acknowledge not knowing how to comfort or console you? Did they seek forgiveness? Were they able to demonstrate their desire to respond with more attention and care moving forward?

Every parent fails—but the worst failure is not addressing the failure. At times, a parent can be willfully blind to the harm they cause. At other times, parents can address their failures by requiring the child to exonerate them and tell them how wonderful and loved they are. In either case, the truth is not being engaged, and the child is left feeling alone and likely blaming themselves for what is not their fault.

With these categories in mind, return to the data you gathered from the four scenes and answer these questions:

1. How did you learn to manage what you felt was not addressed well by one or both parents? How did you soothe yourself? What did you do with hurt and anger?
2. What was your role in your family, and what behaviors were required to keep your role in place? How did that role differ from your siblings'? What happened when you failed to perform your role as was implicitly required?
3. Was your style of engaging your family more fight, flight, freeze, or fawn?
4. What sensitivities developed in your way of engaging the world and relating to others from what you have discovered?
5. What have you learned about your story that now seems more understandable and heartbreaking? And what can you learn from your spouse's story that now seems more understandable and heartbreaking?

These five questions are an invitation to consider your response to trauma and your triggers. We will spend more time on your crucial issues now that you have done some hard work in exploring your family of origin and how it shaped you.

Dig deeper with us in the video series using the QR code at the back of the book.

Part 3

Understanding How You Relate

Your story, and how it intersects with your spouse's story, holds the key to growing deeper, stronger roots in your marriage. The thought of reviewing your past might trigger you to want to stop reading—and if that's what you need, then take a deep breath and come back to this exploration later. Or you may have already spent considerable time and intentional effort looking at your story. You may enjoy the process and have many memories upon which to reflect.

Regardless of where you are on the spectrum of responses, you are in a unique vantage point with a fresh opportunity to consider events, relationships, and circumstances—and your reactions, assumptions, and conclusions to them—that have shaped you. And until you begin the hard work of truth telling and framing your story from a larger perspective of potential wholeness, you likely won't discover the most important themes your story can reveal.

Left unobserved and unaddressed, your story will continue to manifest certain themes and patterns in your life. The good news, however, is that you can intentionally change your story—not change the past but gain deeper understanding of its impact on you and change how you respond to its impact as you move forward.

Here are some big ideas we will explore in Part 3:

- Denial or avoidance of what is true in our stories inevitably brings about more harm.
- Our family of origin sets the baseline for how we handle trauma and, along with other key experiences, forms our trauma responses.
- Emotional trauma involves two primary categories: loss and humiliation. Each carries layers that, combined and compounded by other kinds of trauma, tend to bind us in fear, shame, and contempt.
- Physical trauma encompasses threats of harm, bullying, and violence inside as well as outside our family of origin's home, often blended with emotional violations and humiliation.
- Not everyone has been sexually abused, but no one has escaped sexual harm, including the hurtful cultural messages and conditioning done by families, peers, and churches.

3.1

What's Your Story?

It is never too late to care for the body, soul, and heart. It is never too late
to become the person you're meant to be and to love your partner with
more ferocity and joy. It is never too late to tend to your trauma.

THE DEEP-ROOTED MARRIAGE, P. 60

Live your story or your story will live you.

Perhaps you've heard this anonymous koan-like adage before. You might nod in agreement or find that it rings hollow with an echo of cliché. Regardless, it expresses a certain truth about the significance of looking with curiosity, compassion, and courage at the events of your life and the way they have shaped the kind of person you are and how you live your life. Because if you don't explore your story, parts of it will influence how you think, feel, choose, and act, often without your conscious awareness.

You might also recall that Socrates famously said, "The unexamined life is not worth living," pointing out the necessity of examining your life in search of meaning and significance. Without grasping some idea of who you are and where you come from, it's challenging to control where you go next. We see variations of this truth throughout history, both socially and politically, individually and nationally. It permeates literature from Greek tragedies to postmodern novels, from biblical narratives to superhero origins. And it continues to emerge as fundamental to recovery and healing for any human being overcoming life's traumas.

Understanding your story is not only required for personal transformation and wholeness, but if you and your spouse wish to experience the taste of heaven available in your union, then understanding each other's story is just as paramount. Only as you develop a more accurate perspective on the impact of your stories coming together will you be able to change the ruts pulling you apart.

Most of us tend to ignore our past harm and try to escape it—at times, even unknowingly—which ultimately worsens and multiplies it. But knowing better how to make different choices in the heat of the moment begins with simply knowing. You can choose either to sit in the discomfort of honesty and humble acknowledgement of your pain now or to go on deepening and spreading your heartache. As a counseling client once put it, "I'm learning that I either pay now, or I pay even more later."

You get to choose.

- If your life story thus far were made into a Netflix docuseries, how would it be described for viewers? Or if a film were based on your life, what genre would it be—comedy, action, suspense, horror, mystery, romance? Something else?
- What three words describe what rises up in you as you anticipate looking at your story and its impact with greater scrutiny? Why those three words?

Breaking the Surface

Some of the most impactful catalysts in your life are probably easy to identify—your parents' divorce, illness or injury, moving, switching schools, loss of a loved one, your first job. Others, however, may have been overlooked or dismissed as trivial or relatively inconsequential, which in turn minimizes your ability to see the trail of collateral damage they caused in your life. In order to help you explore both familiar wounds and those more subtle, and often insidious, in their harm, you may find it helpful to recall how you are made.

Simply put, you are meant for honor and delight.

You were designed to be treated with genuine care and respect. To encounter people and places that stir profound awe and joy in you. To experience the beauty and intimacy of Eden.

Today, of course, you are no longer in the original Eden of the past or the restored Eden of the future. Although you can catch glimpses of that abundant beauty, you—along with the rest of us—live in what theologians call the "already and not yet." While the kingdom of God is here now, its consummation—the full restoration of the earth and all who live in it—has yet to occur. And in this era of the "in-between," we all know suffering. We all experience trauma.

At times you may be tempted to define your life primarily by the pain, loss, and trauma you've experienced. Or you may have always been able to enjoy the glare of the bright side, finding silver linings in even the darkest, most tarnished experiences. Whether you live with an awareness of your life's traumas front and center 24/7 or attempt to focus only on glimmers of goodness and hope, you have suffered, and it continues to affect your life—and your marriage.

The good news, though, is that you don't have to suffer your traumas continuously, and you can in fact do better than simply looking for silver linings. Your trauma does not have to become the undoing of you. Nor does your spouse's trauma have to rob you both of the joy possible in growing deeper roots as you experience and facilitate healing with one another.

You can walk the path of healing, know deep connectedness, even experience transformation—if only you will address your trauma with brave honesty and consistent care. There is pain, yes; but there is also hope for beauty, meaning, and joy. You have the option of inviting the kingdom of God into your deepest places.

- Look back for a moment at your responses to the exercise and questions at the end of Part 2 in Nourishing the Roots (section 2.3). What has lingered or stayed with you most since completing that exercise involving the four scenarios? What emerged that continues to surprise you?

- When you consider that you were made for honor and delight, for respect and genuine care, what thoughts pop up? What emotions emerge? What are you aware of feeling in your body?

- Complete the following sentence: "When I consider that my marriage has the potential to change the impact that past trauma has on my life, I immediately think _____ _____ because _____ _____ ."

- On a scale of 1 to 5 (with 1 being "little to no awareness" and 5 being "great or complete awareness"), how would you rate your present understanding of the role past trauma has had in shaping your story? What's the basis for your rating?

- Similarly, using the same scale of 1 to 5, how aware are you currently concerning the impact of past trauma on your spouse's story? What's the basis for your rating?
- If you are ready, share your answers with your spouse. Aim to let this prompt curiosity, not criticism; discussion, not debate.

Letting In the Light

The word trauma is now used with more and more frequency. You are likely to find it in a variety of daily contexts: news articles, social media posts, podcasts, films and TV, human resource policies, sermons, your doctor's office, therapist's office, book club, small group, and confidential conversations with friends. Like any word that floods the mainstream banks of language use, the meaning of trauma has evolved.

Derived from the Greek, *trauma* literally means "wound" or "wounding." When emergency room medics or first responders assess incoming patients, they prioritize by the severity of trauma. Not all trauma, however, is physical or even visible. Various kinds of trauma may go undetected or remain present in subtle ways before manifesting in more overt ways when triggered by a catalyst.

You may not feel the word *trauma* applies to your story, that it relates only to damage more severe than your own. The truth, though, is that you have known harm, whatever the severity. Until now, you may have failed to identify and acknowledge trauma and its impact on your story for a number of reasons. But as you begin looking more closely at past trauma in your life, allow yourself to consider it in broad terms:

> *Trauma is any violation of human dignity that comes through emotional, physical, sexual, or spiritual harm.*
> *Trauma desecrates what was meant to be, leaving the person feeling fragmented, numb, and isolated.*
> *Trauma in all its forms leaves a residue that mars our sense of self and way of relating to others.*

With these parameters in mind, you likely recognize that some harm appears subtle and insignificant (usually called "small-t trauma"), whereas other events are overtly and obviously violating ("capital-T trauma"). Most people generally fail to see small-t trauma and diminish the importance of what they intuitively know left scars. And even when capital-T trauma cannot be ignored or denied, its impact remains confusing and unpredictable.

Maybe you feel hesitant to name and address trauma. You might have had wonderful parents, and nothing major stands out to you. Even so, try to remain curious, even if it is uncomfortable or seems pointless. Your parents may have done their best, but you likely will still find areas in your life where you felt unseen, fearful, or hurt without comfort. Heavy burdens are sometimes inadvertently placed on young children for the family's survival. Sometimes generations of harm and trauma have trickle-down effects that are unexpected.

Naming your trauma can feel harsh, judgmental, and dishonoring to those who raised you. But the goal here is not to cast blame; it is to explore the impact of your experiences and how they have shaped you.

Living Water

The way you respond to trauma largely results from how your family of origin conditioned you to respond to it. Your parents or primary caregivers set a baseline around which your responses to trauma evolved. Other experiences and forms of trauma then shaped the assumptions you made and absorbed the defensive strategies required for survival.

Generally, these traumatic experiences involve emotional, physical, or sexual abuse. This triad often overlaps like a Venn diagram with the most traumatic experiences involving all three. Nonetheless, experiences isolated to one sphere are sufficient to cause significant rupture without overlap or reinforcement from other incidents of abuse.

There is no easy, one-size-fits-all healing process for each dimension of trauma, especially for those that overlap. Transformation, however, begins with cultivating and practicing the gifts of attunement to your grief and anger. You need a witness who both feels the sorrow of what you suffered and is incensed by the injustice of what you endured. You need tenderness and righteous anger.

This is the dual response often emerging from the pages of the Scriptures. One striking example is the life of Joseph as recounted in the Old Testament. From the beginning of his life, Joseph endured the burden of being his father's favorite, which in turn resulted in his brothers' hatred: "Now Israel loved Joseph more than any of his other sons, because he had been born to him in his old age; and he made an ornate robe for him. When his brothers saw that their father loved him more than any of them, they hated him and could not speak a kind word to him" (Genesis 37:3–4).

Of course, Joseph didn't help matters by sharing his prophetic dreams of grandeur with his brothers. Their jealousy and rage boiled into a murderous plot to kill their brother and deceive their father about the death of his favorite son. Instead, they sold Joseph into slavery to a traveling group of Midianite merchants passing through. But they maintained their conspiracy to lie to their father, dipping Joseph's coat of privilege in goat's blood and leading their father to believe their brother had been devoured by a wild animal (Genesis 37:12–36).

Favoritism, exponential sibling rivalry, betrayal, physical harm, intent to kill, and trafficking—quite the capital-T trauma checklist, and Joseph's story had only begun. As you may recall, Joseph went on to endure sexual assault as the prey of Potiphar's wife, only to be accused, arrested, and incarcerated as the perpetrator of sexual harm against the scorned seductress (Genesis 39:6–20).

Helped by his gift for interpreting dreams, Joseph wound up advancing, against all odds, to become Pharaoh's second-in-command. Under Joseph's leadership and strategic planning, Egypt maximized the years of abundance to prepare for the famine that followed—the same famine that struck Joseph's Hebrew homeland and caused his brothers to show up begging for food (Genesis 42).

After so many years, they didn't recognize Joseph in his new role. And after a bit of back-and-forth with his brothers, including some toying with their fears and guilt, Joseph not only fed them but forgave them and was reunited with his father (Genesis 42–50). After their father died, Joseph's brothers once again feared his revenge and retaliation. Instead, Joseph explained how he managed to endure a lifetime punctuated with virtually all forms of trauma:

When Joseph's brothers saw that their father was dead, they said, "What if Joseph holds a grudge against us and pays us back for all the wrongs we did to him?" So they sent word to Joseph, saying, "Your father left these instructions before he died: 'This is what you are to say to Joseph: I ask you to forgive your brothers the sins and the wrongs they committed in treating you so badly.' Now please forgive the sins of the servants of the God of your father." When their message came to him, Joseph wept.

His brothers then came and threw themselves down before him. "We are your slaves," they said.

But Joseph said to them, "Don't be afraid. Am I in the place of God? You intended to harm me, but God intended it for good to accomplish what is now being done, the saving of many lives. So then, don't be afraid. I will provide for you and your children." And he reassured them and spoke kindly to them.

GENESIS 50:15–21

Read the biblical passage above once more and underline or circle any words or phrases that jump out at you. Then use the following questions to think through your observations and relevant implications.

- Which forms of abuse and trauma do you have in common with Joseph in this passage? Are there any ways that his family dynamic reminds you of your own? How so?
- What words or phrases did you underline or circle? Why do they resonate with you and your story?
- If you had been in Joseph's place all those years later when his brothers showed up, how would you have handled your reunion? What would you have wanted to say to them?
- Do you believe God is always committed to healing and redeeming the harm we experience? Why or why not?

Sharing Fruit

You are encouraged to identify at least one major kind of trauma—emotional, physical, sexual—in your story in order to trace its traumatic impact and collusion with relational dynamics, including your spouse's story. We will begin with emotional trauma since it always accompanies the other two categories of abuse. Emotional trauma often pivots between loss and humiliation.

In the context of your story, loss involves significant grief that has been plastered over because your parents could not contain sorrow and remain intact, usually resulting in being overwhelmed by it (and needing to numb or escape it) or detaching and dissociating from it. Humiliation results from being shamed for your body, face, clothing, mannerisms, speech, or actions and consequently estranged and emotionally isolated from those with whom you wanted connection.

Where in your story have you experienced loss? Abandonment? Rejection? Dislocation? Divorce? At first, write a few sentences about where you have known significant loss. Then, find a quiet place to close your eyes and picture the scene, the stage, the actors in the story, the dialogue or absence, and what was required of you at that moment. What has lingered in you that continues to handle loss in a similar way?

Don't fight against what you don't remember. You don't need to swear in court that each detail is accurate without doubt or equivocation. Remember, if it is a traumatic event, the story is likely fragmented with many details forgotten or erased. All you are doing is allowing your imagination to see what could have happened, given that you know the people and how the plot likely ensued. Be willing to trust yourself.

Humiliation is usually reductive and belittling and sets you up to feel like a fool. So think back for a few moments: Where have you felt like a fool? When were you the object of derisive laughter and mockery? Who were the mockers? What was said? What was it like to see the face of disgust or contempt? Where did you go? How did you attempt to escape or minimize the humiliation?

You are now deep in the realm of shame. Humiliation is shameful. To experience shame from decades ago will trigger denial, minimization, dissociation, or self-soothing behaviors that may have worked to some degree but bring about more harm today. For example, are you inclined once you begin to do this work to eat, drink a glass of wine, vacuum an already clean floor, pick a fight with your spouse, social media scroll, or lose track of time?

Notice that we can't address shame well without safety and kindness. What does it mean to be kind—tender and strong on behalf of the younger part of you that endured loss and/or humiliation? What can you do to tend to what is stirred up in you that doesn't bring more harm and offers your body and soul fierce tenderness?

One practice to help you face the impact of loss and humiliation in your life is to become more cognizant of emotional triggers. These explosions are triggered whenever you overreact disproportionately to lesser harm. You may gravitate toward fight, flight, freeze, or fawn, but the triggered response doesn't equal the apparent catalyst.

You'll recall my (Dan's) example from Part 2 about my wife correcting my choice of cooking oil for a stir-fry. My initial internal response to Becky suggesting I not use olive oil triggered a long history of feeling incompetent and stupid. Her suggestion was not the issue—it was my sensitivity to humiliation.

3.2

What's Your Operating System?

Our deepest longing is to be cared for. From the moment we are born, we are hardwired to seek and maintain the presence of a caregiver, to be nourished physically and emotionally. We need someone to be attuned to us, to respond to our emotional and physical needs.

THE DEEP-ROOTED MARRIAGE, P. 63

A buse is always traumatizing whether we own the wounds or not. Often compounding and complicating the impact of trauma is the fact that abuse is seldom isolated from other forms of harm. A person who was sexually abused was also likely harmed emotionally, physically, and spiritually. Bullying is both emotional and physical and often degrades the victim's sexual identity. Physical abuse seldom occurs without emotional abuse, just as spiritual abuse always involves some degree of emotional violation.

If every form of abuse distorts our sense of self and approach to others, we need to find out how that is playing out for us personally. You have already started this process with the courage to reflect, the willingness to be curious, and the resolve to truly understand your own story. You are learning to accept your humanity fully and kindly.

And you are so much more than your trauma—it does not get to name you or define you. Take heart as you continue because your effort to gain awareness will ultimately take you somewhere new. You're addressing your past harm in order to manage it and keep it from bringing more present harm. You're positioning yourself for true healing and intimacy.

How does this transformation take place? By first looking at your story and the trauma you have experienced—and then by studying your reactions to trauma and the coping strategies you learned in order to survive. As these strategies blended with other aspects of your personality and experiences, you formed an operating system, a way of relating to protect yourself from more harm.

Unfortunately, operating systems tend to become default rather than deliberate and often hinder the growth and intimacy you crave. The good news is that operating systems formed by your past can be re-formed today. As you learn to identify the components of your operating system, you gain new understanding about what keeps trying to come between you and your spouse.

- What past trauma or aspect of your story has been the most challenging to recall and explore so far? What has it stirred up in you?
- What comes to mind when you hear the term "operating system"? What are some other descriptors or names you might give this way of relating you've developed based on past trauma and life experiences?

Breaking the Surface

Your deepest longing is to be cared for. From the moment you were born, you were hardwired to seek and maintain the presence of caregivers, to be nourished physically and emotionally. You are not alone in your innate neediness—all human beings are born needing someone to be *attuned* to them, to respond to their emotional and physical needs.

If you had a caregiver who consistently responded to your needs as a child, you developed a sense of security and safety, a connection that soothed your distress, calmed your fears, and provided reassurance. You experienced attunement. You established a secure attachment to parents or caregivers.

Like many people, however, your experience with those responsible for your care may have been something quite different. Perhaps they were unavailable, distracted, absent, or inconsistent, leaving you confused and disoriented, and you developed strategies to survive relationally. You experienced a lack of attunement—and lacked the secure attachment you were made to enjoy.

Attune means to "bring into harmony." It is the capacity to "tune into" other people, simply being aware of them and their feelings. It's communicating care to someone by offering your presence and focus. Listening with full attention. Letting them know you get it. Interacting in a way that reassures their heart they are seen and cared for.

When an attuned caregiver responds to the distraught cries of a child, the child is soothed and comforted. If this happens consistently, a child's needs become less distressing for them. They trust their needs will be met by their caregiver.

When a caregiver is not attuned with a child and does not meet his or her needs, the child learns that communicating anguish is unlikely to bring a response. Children in those situations may come to believe, *No one is interested in meeting my needs. There is no one I can trust to nurture, protect, and care for me. Now I must find a way to cope.* When their own needs rise up in them, they bury them, desperate to avoid the painful neglect, or even aggravation, of their caregivers. They usually determine a way to get what they need on their own. Expressing their needs to an unattuned caregiver becomes simply unbearable. Better to distance oneself from the need or get what they can on their own than experience the pain of neglect, lack, and deprivation.

When you did not receive the care you needed throughout your childhood, you adapted brilliantly in order to survive. You used your earliest experiences, especially those involving trauma, to create ways of coping to get the comfort, care, affirmation, and security you inherently needed. You suppressed some needs and learned to meet others in ways that felt within your control.

These ways of coping, which we call an operating system, ironically create challenges to your present pursuit of intimacy because they sound the alarm based on past experiences. You are no longer reliant on caregivers for your needs—you have agency to meet those needs, express them to others, and receive healthy fulfillment. Without an intentional update in your operating system, however, you will continue to let the past interfere with your present.

- How would you describe the circumstances around your birth and infancy based on what you have been told or discovered? How did these circumstances affect the ability of your parents or caregivers to attune to your needs then?
- Similarly, think about your earliest memories and the experiences they involve. What stands out about the way your caregivers responded to your needs? What messages did you receive from them about your needs?
- Often, one's earliest physical needs—for food and water, warmth and shelter, cleanup and

fresh diapers—may have been met while emotional needs for comfort and soothing, security and consistency went unmet. Would you agree that your physical needs were met more thoroughly and consistently than your emotional needs when you were a child? Why or why not?

- Looking back at your childhood, were you fairly independent and self-sufficient? Or did you rely on others more and get anxious about their ability to provide what you needed?
- Based on your knowledge of your story and its earliest years, place a check next to the statements below that are true of your experience.

_____ Virtually all my needs, both physically and emotionally, were met by my caregivers, and I knew I could always count on them.

_____ Most of my physical needs were met, but my emotional needs were often ignored, minimized, or stigmatized by shame.

_____ All my emotions were acknowledged and validated by my caregivers, and they provided guidance about how to express them in healthy ways.

_____ My emotional and psychological needs for worth, value, and significance were provided by one parent or caregiver more than the others. This caregiver was:

_____

_____ At some point early on, I concluded that my needs were not that important, so I rarely expressed them or asked for what I needed.

_____ Attunement by my caregivers allowed me to enjoy security and a sense of confidence that my needs would be met.

_____ My caregivers were too distracted with other concerns to notice and meet my needs on a consistent basis.

_____ As I matured into adolescence and adulthood, I learned to meet my own needs rather than look to others—including my spouse—to meet them.

Letting In the Light

It is a crucial task to look squarely at abuse, to understand it, identify it, and track its impact—but it is weighty. Sometimes excruciating. As we process these hard realities, let's come back to a few bigger, unchanging truths that we can count on no matter what we have been through.

You and I were made in the image of God; we have his imprint on us.

He infused us with immense value and dignity.

He chooses to dwell in us.

He invites us into the joyful, loving community of the Trinity.

He intends us to experience honor and delight.

He names us his beloved.

Even as we may feel far from these beautiful realities, he wants to draw us into them. He relentlessly reaches out to his beloved; he doesn't leave us to be permanently damaged.

With that knowledge, we can move toward the path of healing simply by gaining new awareness. Continue to focus on building awareness of where you've been—and the role of past trauma in how you operate in the present. What is the story you lived? Go back to all the younger versions of you. What troubling emotions stand out? When were you conflicted, frustrated, or hurt? What left you feeling small, humiliated, or violated?

It is also helpful to consider what you have given to others but not received yourself. We often are far better to our children and friends than we are to ourselves. It is crucial for you to see how, in the brilliance of your younger self, you've survived the harm you endured. And you can grieve the harm you endured only to the degree that you approach the harm with a spirit of kindness.

As you continue to acknowledge that you've known harm and to identify its impact, practice the "change agents" of humility and honesty. Sit with what rises up in you. All the while, remember that you are not defined by your trauma. Remember: You are so much more than your trauma. It does not get to name you—or determine your future.

Living Water

Some of your needs likely went unmet during your development into adulthood. Along the way, you reached conclusions that inform the way you relate to yourself, to others, and to God. You formed a self-narrative that evolved as you grew and became reinforced by certain choices you made. Your operating system has its own logic, one informed by the trauma you've experienced and the harm you've endured.

Survival is fundamentally, inherently hardwired into every human being along with having needs. Depending on the patterns formed by your interactions, and lack thereof, with your caregivers, you did what you knew to do in order to both address your needs and ensure your survival. While many variables and nuanced layers form your operating system, two components seem basic to our human nature: shame and blame.

Shame emerges from a sense of being inferior, defective, corrupt, broken, and irredeemable. As you may have learned, shame, distinct from guilt, reflects something flawed about who you are, linking a sense of failure to what you do. You likely absorbed a sense of shame based on the shame your parents and caregivers carried and passed on to you. Perhaps your mother felt shame about her weight or appearance, instilled by her own family of origin, which she then transmitted to you through her critical comments and negative messaging about your body.

Blame is to shame what smoke is to fire. When we experience shame, it often feels overwhelming, all-consuming, and unbearable. So we look for a way to deflect it, release it, and project it onto others by blaming them for the cause of our shame. If we can find someone to blame, then we can alleviate our awareness of our own shame—at least temporarily.

We see both shame and blame operating in the first man and woman mentioned in the Judeo-Christian Scriptures. Given the freedom to make their own choices, and forbidden only one thing in all of Eden, they still succumbed to the wily suggestions of the serpent bent on deceiving them into disobedience. In one sense the serpent's strategy relied on FOMO—the fear of missing out on something so beautiful and delicious, on the opportunity to be greater than themselves and equal to God. But notice what happens as soon as the fruit hit the fan:

> When the woman saw that the fruit of the tree was good for food and pleasing to the eye, and also desirable for gaining wisdom, she took some and ate it. She also gave some to her husband, who was with her, and he ate it. Then the eyes of both of them were opened, and they realized they were naked; so they sewed fig leaves together and made coverings for themselves.
>
> Then the man and his wife heard the sound of the LORD God as he was walking in the garden in the cool of the day, and they hid from the LORD God among the trees of the garden. But the LORD God called to the man, "Where are you?"
>
> He answered, "I heard you in the garden, and I was afraid because I was naked; so I hid."
>
> And he said, "Who told you that you were naked? Have you eaten from the tree that I commanded you not to eat from?"
>
> The man said, "The woman you put here with me—she gave me some fruit from the tree, and I ate it."

Then the LORD God said to the woman, "What is this you have done?"

The woman said, "The serpent deceived me, and I ate."

GENESIS 3:6–13

- You will recall that prior to this incident, the man and woman were "naked, and they felt no shame" (Genesis 2:25). Why do you suppose after eating the fruit their eyes were opened to their nakedness?
- How did the man and woman immediately respond to their awareness of being naked? What do you imagine motivated their response?
- God knew their location yet still asked, "Where are you?" Consider all the things he could have asked them first but did not and write them below.
- How did the shame experienced by the woman and man lead to their shifts to blame? Whom did the man blame? Whom did the woman blame?

After reflecting on your responses to these questions, spend a few minutes in silence before God, considering how you would answer his question, "Where are you?" Ask him to open your eyes to the ways you tend to use shame and blame in your operating system.

Sharing Fruit

If your caregivers failed to provide consistent, caring attunement, then you adjusted your expectations and refocused your strategies for survival. This was not conscious or planned out or deliberate—it was simply your human nature adapting. You realized at an early age that you had to find a way to cope with what you didn't get that you needed—and to overcome the trauma you experienced that you never should have faced.

Attunement trauma is just as real as other forms, even if there was not abuse or severe neglect. Again, it comes back to that inner dialogue: *No one is interested in meeting my needs. There is no one I can trust to nurture, protect, and care for me. Now, I must find a way to cope.* There was relational wounding that left you confused, overwhelmed, or uncertain about where or how to find comfort. It's a result of ongoing unmet needs, and it steered you into a relational pattern that implies intimate relationships are unsafe and unpredictable.

Psychologist John Bowlby, famous for his pioneering work on how infants and children bond or attach to their caregivers, developed the idea of "internal working models," those relational operating systems that our early interactions form in us. We all are "wired" by these lessons; they dictate our assumptions and expectations about how relationships work.

In marriage, our spouse becomes our new "attachment figure," and although we're no longer children, we still seek—or avoid—relational connection in the same kinds of ways. What we couldn't make sense of in our parent in the past creates a similar discomfort and distress in us in the present. We've likely learned to curate how we share, reveal, and express our deepest needs out of fear from past experiences. We want to experience mutual vulnerability with our spouse and cultivate shared intimacy. But we absolutely do not want to experience the pain, disappointment, fear, anxiety, or despair that could happen when we take that risk.

3.3

Nourishing the Roots

Attunement trauma can be so subtle that it is often ignored, minimized,
or dismissed. When it goes unaddressed, it can become the undercurrent
that keeps couples apart. They usually aren't even aware of the
source and feel bewilderingly stuck in their emotional distance.

THE DEEP-ROOTED MARRIAGE, P. 68

This section once again invites you to a more personal exploration and application of the ideas you've encountered in the previous sections as well as *The Deep-Rooted Marriage* book. If you're completing this guidebook with a group, Nourishing the Roots is for you to complete on your own along with your spouse, if they are willing. Of course you're welcome to share your experience doing these exercises with your group at the next meeting, but the primary purpose is to continue growing deeper roots in your relationship with your beloved.

Root-Nourishing Exercise

This root-nourishing exercise continues the process you started at the end of Part 2, which looked at emotional abuse and trauma from your earliest days. We will now consider the impact of physical abuse and sexual trauma in your story and look for a greater understanding about your response to these incidents, relationships, and memories—basically how these contribute to your current operating system.

This exercise may be the most challenging and painful you've undertaken yet, so pay attention to what you're feeling throughout the process along with your body's responses. If you notice you're starting to feel overwhelmed or overly detached, stop and take a break. Get some fresh air, go for a walk, or focus on the details of something nearby through all five senses. Keep in mind that this guidebook and these exercises and questions are no substitute for working with a trained, licensed therapist or counselor.

Physical Trauma

One doesn't have to be physically touched to know physical trauma. The mere threat of being beaten or bullied produces physical trauma. For example, a parent who demands you cut a large enough stick to be used for spanking is combining physical trauma with emotional abuse. The threat conveys that if you don't cut a large enough weapon, you will not only be spanked with one but made to get a more sizable one for more violence. At other times, physical harm without follow-through may have been used to induce fear, but the trauma persists.

Violence Within Your Family

Take a deep breath, hold it, and exhale as slowly as possible. Repeat at least once. Now, think about your experience of physical trauma in terms of violence and bullying within your family. Incidents may be easy to identify, or you may have to look back at more subtle and implicit examples. Consider the following ways violence may have been manifested in your family by answering the questions for each category:

Spanking: Perhaps it's possible, but it's hard to imagine corporal punishment not causing physical trauma. Spanking inherently is intended to inflict physical pain and harm as a consequence, punishment, or deterrent to a child's unwanted behavior. Compounding the trauma, the child may have no idea which of their words or actions will trigger their parents. Or the use of force may seem arbitrary.

- How did you metabolize your parents' anger if you were spanked? Was the punishment excessive, cruel, demeaning, and/or an expression of their frustration with you that exceeded the bounds of dignity? What do you recall feeling at the time? And what feelings rise up in you now?

Physical Abuse: Slapping a child is physically abusive. Making a child sit at a table for an extended period of time for not eating their broccoli is physically abusive. Knocking a child down for hitting his brother is abusive. Burning, cutting, and screaming inches from the face of a child is physically abusive.

- Other than spanking, what forms of physical abuse or traumatic touch did you experience in your home while growing up? Slapping? Kicking? Punching? Dragging? Tickling? Being physically forced to do something? Who in your family tended to perpetrate physical trauma most often? Who tended to experience it most often?

Sibling Vengeance: Sibling rivalry, especially over who is chosen and who is not, who has power and privilege and who does not, provides the basis for both emotional and physical harm. Children sometimes repeat the kinds of physical abuse they experience themselves, and this holds true for siblings. Siblings may also have a keener sense of one another's vulnerabilities. They know how to push one another's buttons.

- If you were older and more physically or psychologically strong, how did you make your siblings suffer your own unresolved heartache? If you were younger and perceived to be weaker, how did your siblings make you pay or fail to protect you? How did your parents respond to altercations between you and your siblings? What messages did you receive about how to survive and endure physical trauma?

Violence Outside Your Family

Sadly enough, violence has become an expected endemic in our world today. From online bullying and social media cancelling to school shootings and attacks at public gatherings, the prospect for violence casts a shadow at the periphery of our cultural consciousness. Anything could happen at any time and anywhere, it seems.

Sports: Contact sports typically involve sanctioned violence that is contained by rules.

In some situations, a coach or team perpetrates excessive and degrading harm for the sake of hazing, "toughening up," or punishing members for poor performance. This problem is often ignored as "just the way it is" rather than being seen as systemic and culturally ignored violence.

- What has been your experience of violence as part of your participation in contact sports? What were the spoken or unspoken physical requirements of being part of the team? What kinds of physical trauma and violence did you perpetuate as part of the team? What kinds were enacted on you?

Racial/Ethnic Degradation: It is common for minority populations, especially people of color, to experience the intersection of emotional and physical threats against their bodies. It is a form of bullying, whether perpetrated by a teacher, a person in authority, a coach, peers on a bus, or strangers in public. Whether it is a microaggression or a direct threat or violation, it weaves identity and trauma into a jumbled mess.

- When have you experienced racial or ethnic degradation or physical trauma? What were the circumstances? What lingering impact has this had on how you view other people? Are you aware of your own cultural and ethnic biases? When have you perpetrated harm, whether subtle and implied or overt and explicit, on others because of their differences?

Bullying: The person perceived to be weak, flawed, or different is inevitably used as an object of ridicule and a scapegoat for violence. Bullying is common, and it is almost inevitable that you were bullied or you were a bully. Bullying usually involves some degree of physical harm, but the mere threat of harm combined with humiliation makes the experience a dark intersection between emotional and physical abuse.

- In what ways were you bullied as a child? In what ways did you bully others while growing up? What lingering impact does bullying have in your operating system? Are you more prone to bully your spouse? Or do you feel like your spouse is more prone to bully you?

Tending to Physical Trauma

There are, of course, multiple steps for tending to physical trauma that are similar to dealing with emotional trauma—but they are also distinct. Here, we will focus on how to tend to physical trauma in the context of your relationship with your spouse—with one major exception: spousal abuse. Obviously, it's impossible to segregate spousal abuse from other forms of physical trauma, but let's start by first looking at how your operating system responds.

Being physically harmed and emotionally demeaned intensifies the natural trauma responses. The fight response becomes more reactive and aggressive; flight becomes quicker and lasts longer. In both fight and flight, there is simultaneously an oversensitivity and a dismissiveness about past harm. More severe harm often creates triggers of freezing that can feel like your spouse is in another world while being able to go about their day with mechanical indifference. When combined with fawning, it might not even be noticed that one's partner has gone deep within a private castle with a wide moat, and the drawbridge is up.

Addressing your own and/or your spouse's past physical abuse requires immense patience because the harm is often blended with emotional violations and humiliation. If the experience of being flooded in the present with the emotions and triggers of past physical harm overwhelms you, consider these guidelines:

Step 1: Go slow. Own your trauma response as yours to address rather than blaming your spouse.

Step 2: Honor your body's response as a gift that enabled you to survive, not as a fault or weakness to blame and shame.

Step 3: Give yourself time—a moment, an hour, or a day—to return to yourself with kindness.

Step 4: Ponder what happened and what themes and scenes are related to this response—first and foremost in your past with your family of origin and trauma events—before you consider past failures with your spouse.

Step 5: Talk about what you have learned and plan what you want to do when this happens again with your spouse to help you feel safe and honored.

Sexual Trauma

Four kinds of sexual trauma need to be considered: (1) family of origin, (2) cultural, (3) sexual abuse, and (4) sexual debris. When we address sexual trauma, it is imperative to know that some of our greatest shame has to do with our sexuality. Sexual abuse often involves emotional and physical abuse, and the collateral damage that comes because of having been abused adds layers of shame and guilt to an already harmed heart. It is as if sexual abuse combines, to a degree, all the other harm into a Venn diagram's inner circle, making it overwhelming to address. It is why sexual abuse seldom gets addressed in marriage, yet it has a devastating impact that affects far more than just our sexual joy.

Family of Origin and Cultural Sexual Trauma

Most families don't talk about sex—other than to say, "Don't." Most churches don't talk about sex other than to reinforce, and often harmfully, God's prescription to wait until marriage. What is often *not* said is that we are genitally self-soothing in the womb. We continue to self-soothe through childhood and eventually discover that self-soothing can elicit strong erotic/sexual feelings that eventuate in an orgasm.

We are told: "Don't have sex. Don't be sexual. Don't think about it. Just wait, and it will all turn out fantastically when you get married." If you do have sex, perhaps you were told you are a ruined flower, a stomped-on birthday cake, a snuffed-out candle. The gratuitous deceit designed to protect wanton youth is, at best, well-intentioned but sets up generation to generation for more shame, secret behaviors, pride, and power plays.

Few, if any, get it right, but it is imperative to consider the dominant themes stated or inferred in your home and church regarding your sexuality. How did these lies or partial truths without a context or narrative shape your sense of sexuality?

- Purity is God's greatest prize.
- If you are sexual, you are dirty, corrupt, and if forgiven, not forgotten.
- Sex is dangerous.
- Girls are responsible for dressing in a way that doesn't tempt boys.
- Boys are more sexual than girls and need protection from their sexual desires.
- Boys will be boys, and their sexual failures are understandable.
- Boys who are sexual are chastised but admired. They are studs.
- Girls who are sexual are cheap, loose, reckless whores.
- The greatest slur is to be called gay or a dyke.

What other spoken or unspoken rules of sexuality and sexual conduct did you absorb growing up? What was the impact on your sexuality then? What is the impact on your sexuality now?

Sexual Abuse

Not everyone has been sexually abused, but no one has escaped sexual harm. Often, we interact with people who tell us they have not been sexually abused but then tell us a story of grooming, exploitation, shame, silencing, or repeated violations.

Let's consider a couple of examples. A young boy is invited into a tree house by older boys whom he admires. He is ecstatic that he has been chosen to be part of the club. Once he arrives, the oldest boy announces that the newest member must undergo an indoctrination process. The first task is to take his clothes off and look at pornography. His young erection is touched and mocked. He is now part of the club. This now-forty-five-year-old man told me he had never been sexually abused. Nothing could be further from the truth.

Similarly, consider a woman in her midfifties who described her adolescent relationship with her stepfather as "playful and flirty." When asked to explain, she shared how he would enjoy embarrassing her by walking around the house in his underwear, often while aroused. He would often comment on her appearance, saying she looked "sexy" if he liked a certain blouse or the way she styled her hair and makeup. Before leaving the house, she would have to give him a kiss on the cheek while aware his hand reached around to rest on her back. When questioned if these acts were sexually abusive, this woman said they were "harmless" because "that's just how men are."

So allow yourself to be curious about how your views of sexuality and particularly your own sexuality and body image have been influenced and harmed. Perhaps the most challenging work is to name sexually violating interactions as sexually abusive. I (Dan) have written about the definition and the implications of harm in two books: *The Wounded Heart* and *Healing the Wounded Heart*. If there is the phenomenon of sexual violation that involves verbal, visual, and physical interaction, then enter this labor to cocreate together new freedom and honor.

The next step is to engage by identifying and generally describing each incident of sexual abuse.

- What experiences occurred that caused you to feel sexually used or violated? It is wise to include any interaction where you felt visually used or violated, as well as times when someone used words to sexualize or objectify you. This also includes interactions where your body was touched for the sexual arousal of an abuser.

As you consider those events, allow yourself to name where it occurred, how old you were, how you were groomed, and what your body suffered and felt during the abuse. You don't have to go into more detail here unless you find it productive, but try to provide an overview of each event, using third person (he, she, they) if helpful.

Writing up to a sentence or two is wise at first. If this is new work, listen well to what your body can bear without growing numb or dissociating. If you find writing to help, then return to write more without asking yourself to write more than you can do with kindness. It is imperative to begin to disrupt shame. It is almost inevitable that shame and contempt remain in your body from decades ago through the judgments you have made against yourself. These are likely being carried on in your sexual and intimate relationship with your partner.

- How have you carried shame and contempt in your body for what your body experienced during the abuse?
- What experiences in your marriage have triggered shame? How have you usually handled shame in these moments? How has your spouse responded?
- How much have you disclosed to your spouse about the various kinds of abuse you have suffered? What has remained unspoken that you want to begin to address?

Dig deeper with us in the video series using the QR code at the back of the book.

Part 4

Connecting the Dots

You may recall learning to connect the dots as a child, eager to prove that you could count just as well as you could draw. Following the progressive sequence of numbers, you moved your pencil from each numbered point to the next, watching an image—perhaps a dog, flower, or house—take shape.

Growing closer to your spouse in shared intimacy can seem similar with one major exception: how you actualize your vision. Instead of the linear, predictable, progressive shift from one point to the next, intimacy in relationship requires a surprising, recursive, creative process of knowing your stories, practicing vulnerability, and creating a unique portrait together. This happens as you see beyond the familiar patterns and tired ruts resulting from your individual trauma responses colliding.

As you connect the relational dots of past and present, you discover a process that's more like a freehand sketch. As artists you can see each other in the present while being aware of the impact of the past. You look and then sketch, capturing one detail on the page and then another, erasing, adjusting, and smoothing lines into curves as you go. There is no formula or one-size-fits-all method. The process is inherently messy and requires patience and perseverance that can be motivated only by love.

Here are some big ideas we will explore in Part 4:

- Insecure attachment, attunement trauma, and self-protection have cumulatively carved patterns of behavior, reaction, and response between you and your spouse.
- Our automatic reactions to threats, real or perceived, involve rapid-fire neurological processes that outpace our capacity for rational, left-brain resolve, resulting in fight, flight, fawn, or freeze.
- While reactivity helps us in moments of physical danger and trauma, it can perpetuate harm in moments of relational tension. This is because our reactivity is often broken; it was formed by the ways we reacted to trauma in the past.
- We connect the dots from past to present by paying attention to what makes us feel unsafe and how we react to it. We can then steer ourselves away from old patterns of perpetual hurt and division and create space for safety, connection, and care.
- Recognizing and changing those patterns that create distance rather than intimacy requires self-awareness, attunement to each other, compassion, forgiveness, and grace.

Dig deeper with us in the video series using the QR code at the back of the book.

How Does Your Operating System
Intersect with Your Spouse's?

*We must be caught more deeply in the realm of story than in the moment of
threat. We can't create space for restoration for our partner or ourselves unless
we know the core stories of heartache and harm from both of our lives.*

THE DEEP-ROOTED MARRIAGE, P. 85

No one pushes your buttons the way your spouse does.
  You might argue that your parents, siblings, or other early caregivers can trigger you
and elicit a quicker, more defensive posture. Perhaps this is true, but it is because of your early
formative experiences of harm and trauma within your family of origin that your most intimate
relationship now suffers. Your reactivity then became your operating system now.

  The reality is that you and your spouse saw something within the other early on that offered
some hope of healing and recovery from past wounding. Unfortunately, however, this magnetic
attraction often becomes a defensive repelling when you don't receive the care you long for and
instead feel more wounded, exposed, and therefore foolish for believing intimacy to be attainable, let alone sustainable.

  Sometimes the spark that ignites tension between the two of you seems to come out of
nowhere. There you are, enjoying a lovely dinner together and relishing the opportunity to get

away from other responsibilities and connect, when suddenly it happens. Your body immediately knows a wire has been tripped, and you feel your pulse accelerate, your shoulders tighten, and your jaw clench. Within moments you think, *Did he really just bring up what we agreed not to discuss again?* Or, *Why would she ask me that right now while we're trying to enjoy a date night?*

Without missing a beat, you shield yourself and shut down, unable to respond and unwilling to engage. You glare and grimace or avert your eyes altogether. Your silence echoes louder than the raised voices you were accustomed to your parents using when you were a child. You go over what just happened in disbelief and regret, having expected to delight in your spouse's company.

Or, on the other end of the spectrum, you might immediately speak without consideration, spewing a shotgun barrage of words intended to retaliate for what you perceive as the unexpected drive-by shot to the heart you just endured. Your spouse responds in kind, and soon you're signaling for the check before you've finished your appetizers. You continue the verbal shooting match, attracting the attention of other diners despite your attempts to contain the volume. There is no way you will allow your spouse to bully you into silence the way your father did with your mother.

Regardless of your response, and whether you have any idea as to why and where and how you learned the response you're giving, this kind of marital combustion often seems inevitable. It might be slow and steady embers sizzling below the surface of safe topics and necessary exchanges or a conflagration of contempt raging with flames that threatens to incinerate you both. Either way, you're caught in a firefight with the person you thought knew and loved you best. Intimacy becomes the casualty, a victim of collateral damage.

Extinguishing such eruptions and resuscitating intimacy requires fire prevention. Sparks may continue to ignite tension at times, and old flames might scorch you occasionally still, but when you learn one another's combustible areas, you can agree not to feed the fire of disconnection, separation, and harm. Instead, you can create a safe space to make different, better choices.

- When was the last time you unexpectedly experienced a rupture in your relationship with your spouse? What was the spark that ignited this fire between you?
- How would you describe the way you typically respond when your spouse says or does something that pushes your buttons? How do these encounters usually resolve?

Breaking the Surface

One of the traditional conventions of the mystery genre is the duality of the plot with one layer revealing what happened leading up to and after the crime or murder and the other, a veneer decorated with false leads, red herrings, and significant clues. Through a process of investigation, research, and forensic examination, the detective then begins peeling away all that obscures the truth, revealing the culprit and the events surrounding the crime. Almost always, the motive behind the crime is uncovered—greed, fear, jealousy, rage, or vengeance.

As you begin connecting the dots between your story and your spouse's, between past trauma and present responses, you become the detective. But in this case, you already know the responsible parties: both you and your spouse. You know the harm that's been done, whether anger and indifference, deception and betrayal, contempt and shame, or worse. You may even think you know what's motivating each of you in how you react and interact with one another in your worst moments.

The big reveal, however, has likely eluded you. Because if you could each see into one another's hearts and minds and understand how the other's reactivity formed, then surely it would alter your own response. There would be a kind of logic revealed that would explain the connection between various incidents and events that harmed your spouse in the past and how he or she coped to survive. You could trace those trauma responses and reactive defenses to your worst moments together and see how your own were triggered.

You could both look back on your years together and see the script you've followed and the dance you've repeated over and over. Even better, you could make direct correlations between the lack of attunement in your relationship and the way it kept you apart, evoking the deep ache of loneliness from the past. The way it tripped your survival strategies as your reactive bodies, unconscious minds, and wounded hearts remembered previous wounds and sounded the alarm. You would notice the times you each dismissed the need for connection and intimacy, convincing yourself your needs were insignificant or could not be met.

If all the layers and labels were removed, the clues would reveal the lies and false assumptions preventing you from coming together. Suddenly the mystery of intimacy would become something to be shared and experienced and no longer a puzzle to be solved. Unlike books and movies, however, this process takes more time and patience, compassion and grace.

- You explored some painful and powerful truths about your story and your spouse's at the end of Part 3 (Nourishing the Roots). Spend a few minutes reviewing your responses and observations about the impact that any form of abuse and trauma has played in your life and your spouse's. What themes and patterns stand out in your work as you consider the big picture? How does recognizing these themes and patterns land with you right now?
- What memories, details, and moments have surfaced in your recent work that surprise you? How have you experienced their impact in your body since uncovering them?
- If you consider the challenges resulting from the way your operating system intersects with your spouse's, how do you see them playing off each other? In other words, how do your trauma responses, based on the past, trigger and fuel your spouse's—and vice versa?
- As you consider all that you have experienced, endured, suffered, and survived, can you also see your strength, courage, resilience, and determination? Describe one example of your response to past harm that illustrates your desire to persevere.
- Similarly, how do you see your spouse's strengths displayed in the ways he or she has endured and survived past harm? What positive quality or trait particularly stands out to you?

Letting In the Light

When relational battles in your marriage wear you down, you're likely tempted to conclude that your needs are the problem. Therefore, it seems safest not to need. If you can convince yourself that your needs are not really that important or maintain the lie that your needs are too over-whelming to be faced, let alone met, by your spouse, then you create a temporary shelter that feels safer than acknowledging and asking for what you need. But it doesn't take long before your needs—and your spouse's needs—begin to surface once again.

Why? Because you are human and needs are fundamental to how we're made. It is healthy and normal to need, to reach out for connection. God saw that it was not good for the first human being to be alone, so he formed an equal yet distinctly different partner. They enjoyed being naked together—not just physically but also emotionally—and were unashamed.

You may have grown up in a home where your needs went largely unmet. Or perhaps your physical needs for food, shelter, and clothing were met while your emotional needs for comfort, security, safety, and attunement were ignored, minimized, neglected, or shamed. You may not consider deprivation as applying to you, but there's a good chance it does if your parents did not see, value, delight in, or protect you. Consequently, you may still have trouble identifying your needs as well as acknowledging them and seeking to have them met in healthy ways. You might hope those needs will simply go away, as shame says it is not okay to need. Or you may tilt more reactively toward self-indulgence by making every whim, desire, or want into a perceived need that must be met.

Often, one spouse tends to sublimate, compartmentalize, or ignore his or her needs while the other's needs get prioritized. We're not talking about the natural give-and-take of supporting one another during the ebb and flow of busy seasons and hectic schedules. No, this dynamic occurs in a marriage when one partner consistently demands more attention and uses whatever means possible to see his or her needs met at the expense of collaborating, compromising, and cooperating with his or her spouse.

You may even set the stage for your spouse's needs to be your primary focus because it's easier to identify and meet his or hers rather than your own. Out of your intense desire for connection, you assume that consistently meeting your spouse's needs will provide the union you crave. You attune yourself to your spouse so that he or she will then rely on you, and value you, notice how loving and supportive you are. Only there's a sense of childlike behavior—"Hey, look at me, aren't I doing a great job?"—displayed by an adult who deeply longs to be seen, noticed, and responded to.

The answer is not denying or burying your needs, nor indulging them above your spouse's. Needs are part of your humanity. But your awareness of them, reaction to them, and attempts at fulfillment can indeed change. Operating systems formed by your past can be re-formed and reshaped today.

Living Water

In order to address the regular issues of life—problems, decisions, conflicts, hurts—with your spouse in a healthy way, help him or her feel free to engage you without fear of judgment or punishment. If one or both of you feel unsafe, some kind of relational fallout is inevitable, even if an issue is resolved quickly. Somewhere down the line, the pattern will repeat, and the buried buildup of hurts from past unsafe moments will rise to the surface.

To steer yourself away from that perpetual hurt and division, you can become more intentional about offering each other kindness and respect in those moments, looking for ways to make room for connectedness and care. Rather than subtle manipulation or overt entitlement, you can communicate directly and respectfully. Instead of assuming and second-guessing your spouse's response, you can open yourself to the possibility that he or she may surprise you. You can listen to what your spouse is communicating rather than simply what is being said—or left unsaid.

These kinds of changes all require a sense of safety—an invitation to speak freely, knowing you will not only be heard but engaged without silencing or belittling. Creating space for safety requires recognizing and understanding what is making you feel unsafe and likely kicking your operating system into overdrive. Only when you feel safe and valued can you hit pause and recognize the opportunity to respond intentionally and not simply react defensively.

We see many striking examples of how well attuned Jesus was to those around him. While we might assume it was easy for him as the Son of God to read minds and hearts, the way Jesus responded to the needs of others reflects his humanity. Jesus defied cultural, religious, and traditional customs and biases in order to engage with others and meet their needs. He knew how to create a safe space for an adulterous woman even in the midst of scheming, self-righteous Pharisees. He surprised the Samaritan woman at the well, not only in respecting her humanity but in helping her acknowledge her spiritual thirst.

One example in particular showcases Jesus' ability to meet people where they were—in this case, his own disciples. After his death and resurrection, Jesus interacted with a number of people, proving his promise to return from the grave had been actualized. Consider for a moment how you might respond to seeing a loved one return to life, someone you saw taking a last breath before witnessing his or her interment; you would certainly be alarmed. Knowing his disciples' fears, doubts, and anxiety about the future, Jesus met them in a safe space and gave them what they needed most.

> Later on that day, the disciples had gathered together, but, fearful of the Jews, had locked all the doors in the house. Jesus entered, stood among them, and said, "Peace to you." Then he showed them his hands and side.
>
> The disciples, seeing the Master with their own eyes, were awestruck. Jesus repeated his greeting: "Peace to you. Just as the Father sent me, I send you."

Then he took a deep breath and breathed into them. "Receive the Holy Spirit," he said. "If you forgive someone's sins, they're gone for good. If you don't forgive sins, what are you going to do with them?"

JOHN 20:19–23 MSG

- What stands out to you about the way Jesus met his disciples where they were, literally and figuratively? By offering them peace, gifting them with the Holy Spirit, and emphasizing forgiveness, how did Jesus create safety?
- Compare what the disciples likely anticipated with how Jesus surprised them. Considering the example set by Jesus, how does creating safety dispel shame, alleviate fear, and disarm expectations?
- With your spouse in mind, how would you answer Jesus' question, "If you don't forgive sins, what are you going to do with them?"
- On a scale of 1 to 5 (with 1 being "very unsafe and volatile" and 5 being "very safe and secure"), how would you rate the atmosphere between you and your spouse when conflict arises? How would you describe your style of clashing?
- What has to change in order for you and your spouse to create a safe space where you can pause to recognize, acknowledge, and choose how you each will respond to your operating systems? What can you do to create this sense of safety?

Sharing Fruit

Consider something you do frequently that requires little thought, focus, or mental effort, such as driving home from work or school, loading and unloading the dishwasher, sorting and folding laundry, or walking a familiar route through your neighborhood. You've done it so often that you no longer think about how you do it. Your neural pathways have established a channel that allows your body to accomplish the task as if on autopilot, freeing other parts of your brain to focus on other matters.

This ability prevents you from having to rethink how to get home every day or what must be done in order to complete regular chores. In sync with the neural pathways formed by frequent repetition, your body remembers how to complete the smaller movements and master coordination needed to monitor the flow of traffic, turn at the appropriate intersection, and pull into your driveway.

Similarly, you and your spouse have each developed familiar ways of responding and reacting to triggers that your mind and body view as catalysts. While the circumstances, events, and people may differ, some aspect of certain moments caused alarm and an immediate shift into red-alert status. Basically, your body and brain are hardwired for survival and evaluating threats, whether real or perceived, with rapid-fire processes that exceed your rational left brain's ability to assess, analyze, and resolve. Once your stress biochemicals and neurological reactivity crash your systems, you go into flight, fight, fawn, freeze—or some combination thereof.

We all are a complex mosaic comprising the same tiles but in vastly different trauma configurations, and it is impossible to know which tiles result from genetics and which from learning. Many people immediately respond to a threat with flight, fleeing from the danger and turning to other activities to help restore order to their external and internal worlds. Some people avoid tensions in their marriage by resorting to work. Others clean, garden, binge-watch screens, cook, read, or exercise.

Many people also respond to the anxiety of a threat with an anger-fueled desire to fight. They're consumed by a sense of injustice: *this is wrong and should not be; therefore, I must fight back*. Once our anxiety gets triggered, anger mobilizes and activates our will to overpower or intimidate the threat.

Rather than experiencing anxiety, some people cope with trauma by dissociating. When they suddenly encounter something terrible, they often can't speak or move and may even faint. Like an electric charge shorting out a fuse, they freeze when a threat radically overwhelms their neural pathways. Thought and feeling shut down to disconnect from the present danger of reality and may last for moments, hours, or even longer.

The other primary form of avoidance is fawning—resolving tension by stifling emotion, pleasing others, and trivializing the problem rather than addressing it. Fawning is also called *chronic compromise* or letting others make decisions. It usually involves camouflaging ourselves to escape notice. We cover up our anxiety, anger, fear, and sadness by smiling, laughing, cracking jokes, or drastically changing topics.

How Does Your Operating System Impede Intimacy?

Curiosity is foundational to emotional intimacy. It says, I want to see you. I want to know you. I want to be with you. Curiosity reminds us that our partners chose us — and are still choosing us. Curiosity is an intentional engagement with our spouses. Curiosity reminds us that we matter. It offers a sense of presence to our spouses.

THE DEEP-ROOTED MARRIAGE, P. 131–132

Humans are association-making beings, tending to make pairings with events. When fear and anxiety get triggered, you react based on how you've learned to react and survive when faced with past threats. Rarely without intentionality do you stop and think, *I wish my spouse had not spoken unkindly just now. He knows I'm sensitive about my weight. His comment seems like covert shaming. I wonder if that was his intention?* No, instead you immediately react!

Depending on the variables that have shaped and chiseled the ways you react to a threat, you might jump right into anger. You might express outrage and try to deflect your own shame, hurt, and pain onto your spouse: "Way to go. Thanks for calling me fat! Because that's what you're saying. Well, have you stepped on the scale lately? You should try that next time before you lash out at me!"

Or perhaps when your spouse makes a comment that immediately stings, you shut down your emotions and disconnect from your body. You might ignore his or her words and quickly change the topic to something benign and safe. You might make a self-deprecating joke and crack a smile. You might thank your spouse for caring about your appearance and (indirectly) encouraging you to lose weight.

Whatever your matrix of responses—and they can differ depending on what and by whom and how you were triggered—you don't stop and think: you just react. And you keep doing it.

And you're not alone because we all do a version of this. Today, we inhabit the same body that experienced fear, hurt, and shame in our early years; our body *knows* where we have been every day of our lives. While we may not spend time consciously thinking about our past painful experiences, our bodies remember them, no matter how long ago they occurred. And when we feel it all over again, we react, sometimes in surprising ways. *And we keep doing it.*

We're instinctively seeking safety to protect ourselves, just as we did when we were younger. Our bodily reactions are natural and necessary, and they give cues about the ways we need care and what deeper hurts need tending. But they're also reactions we can slip into repeating without thinking, causing us to pull away from our spouses in the process. Suddenly, intimacy seems far away, if not impossible.

- How do you usually react when you experience something you perceive as threatening from your spouse? Which of the four—flight, fight, freeze, fawn—seems to be your main default response?
- How does your body tend to respond when you feel threatened? What part of your body becomes tense or hurts, goes numb, or feels cold?

Breaking the Surface

As you've likely realized by now, so many of the hot spots within your marriage are merely symptomatic of deeper issues from past trauma within each of you. Your operating systems intersect and create barriers that separate you from the open communication, vulnerable honesty, and shame-free physicality you both were created to enjoy. You want to break free from the pull of the past, but its hold continues to exert gravity when any threat enters your relational atmosphere.

When one of you feels threatened and resorts to anger and retaliation, the other may shut down and start vacuuming every room in the house. Or one partner's anger may serve as an accelerant for the other's, resulting in a volatile escalation neither of you wanted. You might both be conflict-avoidant and respond by fleeing to your respective areas of safety—a bedroom or kitchen, the office or living room, the patio or garage—and then act like nothing happened. Whatever your patterns of reactivity may be, they are keeping you from drawing closer to one another and experiencing intimacy.

Just to be clear, intimacy is not about your sexual relationship and its dynamics—although that usually reflects the emotional distance and level of secure attunement for the two of you. Intimacy is about shared time, space, energy, attention, and attraction. It is the one-flesh union God intended for the first man and first woman, a togetherness of knowing fully and being known fully. It is not only being accepted but delighted in and cherished. Intimacy relaxes the boundaries and stretches the limits of what ultimately separates us from another human being.

Intimacy is not about balanced perfection, which is neither attainable nor sustainable, but instead relies on wholeness, on harmony even in the dissonance of your differences. Intimacy invites and welcomes and celebrates the joining together reflected by your commitment, your presence, your heart-posture, and your body's receptivity. Codependency smothers the other due to the fear of individuation, whereas intimacy blesses difference and honors independence. Intimacy involves mutually meeting needs and promoting growth beyond what is possible for an individual.

Understandably, our past traumas remind us that the risk of intimacy tends to be too great, too costly, too painful. We want to be known and loved, yet we are terrified of being known and loved and the risk that requires. Marriage defies the logic of our default defenses by daring to hope that love can achieve intimacy despite any and all barriers erected by ourselves and by our pasts.

Without a doubt, we all have some kind of wounding, and we all will be triggered at times. It's not that these moments ought not occur; what matters is how we respond to them.

Will we be aware of our default reactions and be honest about them with our partners? Are we willing to reengage and reconnect, even when our bodies remember a familiar pain? Also, will we choose to look closer with curiosity when our partners are triggered? Will we offer them emotional presence, listen, validate their struggles? Will we imagine a new way to move forward together?

It's in these marriage moments that we have the opportunity of a redemptive experience, the chance to move toward intimacy as we close the distance between us. With our partners, we can disrupt the old patterns and create new stories in the present.

- What are some of the hot spots or recurrent issues that block intimacy with your spouse? When was the last time you experienced one of these barriers?
- How would you describe the dance between you and your spouse when one of you triggers the other? How does each of you usually behave when a threat tries to sever your attunement to one another?
- How would you define or describe intimacy as you've experienced it so far with your spouse? What would it look like for you to experience greater intimacy in your marriage?
- Do you agree that your sexual relationship reflects the level of intimacy between you and your spouse rather than determining it? Why or why not?
- Complete this sentence: "The greatest barrier to intimacy in my marriage right now is ___ _____ as evidenced by _____ _____."

Letting In the Light

With the couples we (Dan and Steve) counsel, we often see them caught in cycles of reenactment, and we experience it in our own marriages as well. It's a familiar pattern for most of us—a merry-go-round that won't slow down, leaving us stuck as it keeps spinning. Until we learn how to jump from it.

To move toward disrupting this cycle, we have to step back and see what keeps us going round and round, recognizing the hurtful dynamic we're creating as we relate based on past harm. Typically, we experience something that triggers a felt experience of a past trauma. Then, we naturally reenact behaviors that have, in the past, enabled us to survive such heartache—but these are not productive in the present.

Instead, they lead to defensiveness, accusation, and division. We could even say these self-protective rituals bring psychological sabotage into our partner dynamic. One partner feels so hurt and angry that he or she blurts out severe judgments and vicious accusations. Even if the words bear some truth and resemble reality, they are not spoken for the sake of healing or with any hope of reconciliation. The person is simply exploding his or her frustration and contempt in desperation to find relief.

Each partner thinks, *I was hurt, and I will hurt you in response. I will make you pay for the harm done to me.* This is how reenactments are justified and reinforced.

The reenactment of feeling triggered and slipping into survival strategies happens nearly as fast as the speed of sound. Once the process begins, it is like stumbling. You can know you are beginning to fall and wish you could self-correct, but gravity takes hold, and it is impossible to ground yourself firmly. Usually, the best you can do is minimize the impact of the fall. Tragically, few of us know how to fall well without getting hurt or knocking into someone else.

Each couple is telling some truth in their reflection of a marriage conflict yet taking little to no ownership of their part in the tension.

Judgment is contempt that condemns without considering context and disguises and defends our part in the problem. Such judgment against our partners and ourselves is like a cloud preventing us from being able to see what's happening. In these moments, judgment is a way we cope with pain. It temporarily protects us and relieves us from the hurt we feel—yet it reinforces the reenactment cycle.

Living Water

Knowing at a logical, executive-functioning level that our self-protective behaviors lead to more harm, unfortunately, does not mean we'll stop doing them. Even if we "just try harder" to avoid doing them, we usually only build momentum for an even greater crash at a later point.

Your goal cannot be simply to remove reenactments, triggers, damage, and shame from your life—this is not doable. You, along with all of us, will continue to wrestle with these thorns just as we wrestle with sin for the rest of our lives.

Our triggers are so deeply embedded in our brains and bodies that to erase the source would be to erase the mind. Shame alerts us to matters that are core to who we are and who we are meant to become. The goal is to become quicker to engage the trigger and clearer on how to disrupt the process of reenactment so we can open ourselves up to healthier responses, healing, connection, and intimacy.

To do this, we need to identify what our bodies remember and engage with our trauma stories, which takes great courage. The more we can enter our own stories of harm with kindness, the more attuned we can be to our spouses' shame cycles. And the more the process is a shared privilege and calling, the more likely it is that kindness will repeatedly interrupt the cycle and leave us open to the work of healing.

This shared endeavor toward intimacy requires that your love for one another grows deeper roots and matures. In the midst of struggling to break the reenactment patterns that often seem so deeply embedded, you can find encouragement by recalling what's true. And what's true in your marriage is a divine, purposeful union that can defy the logical, probable odds as you experience healing.

With this goal in mind, read the familiar scriptural excerpt below and allow yourself to reflect on it with fresh eyes. If this poetic passage has become trite or clichéd, consider inserting the first-person plural pronouns "we" and "our" in order to make its universal description of love more personal and intimate. Use the questions after the passage to take your personal application even further.

Love is large and incredibly patient. Love is gentle and consistently kind to all. It refuses to be jealous when blessing comes to someone else. Love does not brag about one's achievements nor inflate its own importance. Love does not traffic in shame and disrespect, nor selfishly seek its own honor. Love is not easily irritated or quick to take offense. Love joyfully celebrates honesty and finds no delight in what is wrong. Love is a safe place of shelter, for it never stops believing the best for others. Love never takes failure as defeat, for it never gives up.

Love never stops loving.

1 CORINTHIANS 13:4–8 TPT

- At this point in your journey through this guidebook, how would you describe or restate the goal of removing barriers to intimacy in your marriage? What aspect of this process remains unclear or challenging?
- What came to mind when you realized this passage was from the well-known overview of love found in 1 Corinthians 13? What's your history or associations with this passage?
- Read through the passage once again, slowly. Underline or circle any words or phrases that stand out or strike a chord with you and your marriage. What rises up in you as you consider allowing this passage to help move you toward greater intimacy in your marriage?
- What does it look like for you to make love a "safe place and shelter" in your relationship with your spouse? How does love fuel your ability to persevere in your marriage?

After reflecting on your responses to these questions, consider spending a few minutes in silence before God, seeking his presence in the ways you and your spouse love each other. Invite him to open the eyes of your heart so that you can experience a deeper love for your partner and greater wisdom about how to grow closer.

Sharing Fruit

Judgment and justification often form a foundation around which other emotional debris clings, forming multilayered reenactment defenses. But what if we could take judgment out of the equation? It takes a tremendous amount of courage to do this amid tension, but let's imagine it for a moment and see how much more room for curiosity and honesty we'd have. Consider the last time you and your spouse experienced reenactment in some form and think about how the interaction would have been different if judgment had not been in the mix.

Removing the cloud of judgment enables us to see more of what's really going on. But gaining this type of awareness is only the first step toward change.

We often aren't aware that our bodies are remembering something familiar, and our bodies just react. We may not even have words for what we feel. Could we start to awaken to the past hurt we are remembering in the present, to what is causing us to reenact what is familiar?

Sometimes past traumas lie dormant, leaving us unaware of their impact or even how we're feeling them in the present. When you are aware that something is rising up or causing you to react, allow yourself to be curious about what you're feeling and why you might be reacting a certain way. Allow humility to make room for you to see and invite others, such as your spouse or a therapist, to help you see what you cannot discern on your own.

Pushing others away might be easy, but receiving another's care is brave. One choice perpetuates harm, the other invites healing. Sometimes we need to allow others to suffer with us and help us be intentional about remembering the past pains we are carrying.

As you enter intentional remembering, you can create safety and receive reassurance that you can find comfort and kindness, not just more heartache. This is where you can practice giving and receiving attunement and care with your spouse. This is how you close the distance between you and grow in intimacy.

Nourishing the Roots

In humility, we are attuned and aware of what is happening in ourselves and our spouses and aim to disrupt the triggering of trauma, past and present. In honesty, we uncover our own hurts and failures, and own what is ours without blaming our spouses.

THE DEEP-ROOTED MARRIAGE, P. 147

By now you know this final section is designed to facilitate a more personal exploration and application to what you're learning and experiencing. Just a reminder, too, that if you're completing this guidebook with a group, Nourishing the Roots is for you to complete on your own along with your spouse, if he or she is willing. You can choose to share with your group what you take away from these exercises, but their primary purpose is to nourish the roots of your relationship.

This exercise brings together and draws on all of the work, insight, and exploration you have done up to this point. It allows you to practice the process of recognizing your triggers, pausing the reenactment tendencies, and choosing to offer care, curiosity, and kindness to yourself and your spouse. Once again, keep in mind that this is a process, not a formula, for moving beyond the standoff you've often experienced when your operating system collides with your partner's. There is no right way to do this. There is only greater awareness and, therefore, greater freedom to make different choices.

95

Intentional Remembering

Human beings are wired to respond to possible threats as well as what we need in those hard moments. We are designed with deep survival instincts; we look for clues that we're safe, and if we don't sense them, we will seek them out (whether through self-protective, divisive behaviors, or through emotional support from our spouses). We legitimately need a sense of comfort and protection.

Learning to recognize your triggers, and your spouse's, empowers you to hit pause on your reactive response and instead consider how your present reactions are derived from past harm and trauma. This kind of intentional remembering can be painful and challenging and sometimes triggering in itself. But your courage and agency as an adult—drawing on resources and support you did not have when those defensive reactions formed in the past—allow you to see the situation, yourself, and your spouse differently.

As we've said before, as you enter intentional remembering, try to create safety and receive reassurance that you can find comfort and kindness, not just more heartache. Over time, as you realize you are safe and in the present rather than threatened by trauma from the past, you can change course. You can connect more fully to why you and your partner respond the ways you do and how this has tended to create division and isolation. You can learn to identify what your needs are and to ask your spouse for his or hers as well as to provide for yours.

Simply giving and receiving words of reassurance is a powerful antidote to painful memories. Rather than speaking reactively or in retaliation, you can pause and offer a sense of safety and security:

"I get that my abruptness startled you."
"I can see how that impacted you."
"I'll try not to react so harshly."
"I now understand why you tend to respond this way."
"Thank you for seeing me right now."

Awareness is what helps us have a caring response.
Awareness invites understanding, and understanding invites tenderness.
After all, the body is remembering for a purpose; it needs protection and care. It is bringing attention to what requires care and advocating for deep needs to be met.

The goal is to create an atmosphere where we are quick to offer or receive this kind of awareness and tender care at a moment's notice—because our bodies can react in unexpected, even benign moments.

Again, this is not a perfect antidote or a way to avoid challenges that arise. We all will continue to have these kinds of moments in our marriages, no matter how much healing we experience, but we can learn to approach them and move through them in more patient and loving ways.

Flipping the Script

With the goal of awareness, understanding, and tenderness before you, think back on a recent situation, conversation, disagreement, conflict, or emotional pain with your spouse. If you can enlist his or her help in recalling this situation, then you can see a fuller picture, although your spouse's participation is not necessary for this exercise to be helpful. To the best of your ability, briefly describe the location and context for where this incident occurred.

Now, write out the dialogue that was exchanged as accurately and objectively as possible as if you were creating a scene in a play or movie. Try to record what was spoken as well as the body language you recall in yourself and in your spouse. Once you're satisfied that you have a fairly accurate script depicting this incident, take at least a ten-minute break. Get some fresh air, make a cup of tea or coffee, walk around the yard.

When you return, read over what you've written once again and try to analyze it through the lenses you now have at your disposal. Imagine being a film critic or sports analyst offering insight to others about what was going on below the surface during this encounter. Resist the temptation to judge or justify what anyone said or did. Instead, look for ties to past incidents of harm, trauma, and abuse that contributed to what was conveyed during this scene. Insert your insights and revelations into the margins or underneath the script, perhaps something like this:

You: How can you say that I spent too much when you do it all the time?
[Inserted insight: I felt defensive because somehow my emotions and body memory
    went back to times when my parents told me that I wasn't worth spending
    money on.]
Your spouse: Here we go again. You always try and deflect it back on me anytime

we talk about our finances. You refuse to take responsibility for going over budget.

[Inserted insight: I suspect you feel attacked by what I said, which triggers your anger over being the scapegoat in your family whenever things went wrong.]

You: How can I take responsibility when you continue to blame me and never own your part? It doesn't matter. Yes, I'm the problem here, the reason we never stay on budget.

[Inserted insight: I see how I use blame to defend myself by judging you and justifying my going over budget. Then, I felt overwhelmed and disengaged, withdrawing and isolating because I no longer felt safe or seen.]

Once you've inserted your observations and insights, shift your attention to how you and your spouse could flip the usual script and instead create a safe space for mutual care and connection. Consider what you would say now that you didn't say then. Think about what your spouse could have said or done that would have been reassuring, comforting, and safety-promoting. Drawing on your insight and imagination, rewrite your script to reflect a different way of handling the triggers and reenactment tendencies. For example, it might go something like this:

You: I know we need to talk about how much I spent last weekend. But I feel really anxious and jittery about it. Can we just take a minute to catch our breath?

Your spouse: Yes, of course, that's a good idea. I don't want you feeling attacked or accused or judged. We're in this together, and I go over budget just as often.

You: Thank you for saying that. I need to know you're still on my side right now. I appreciate your willingness to help me feel safe.

Perhaps rewriting your script feels awkward, contrived, idealistic, even silly. You might struggle to imagine such a different exchange taking place in the moment when your buttons get pushed and reactivity rises up in you and your spouse. That's okay. Feel free to rewrite your script in a way that seems realistic and feasible to you. But allow yourself to imagine it within a sense of safety and attunement that may have been missing previously.

Self-Attunement

You can practice offering this same compassionate curiosity and care to yourself as you've just imagined in this scene with your spouse. When you feel disoriented or confused about why you feel the way you do, you can begin to attune to what your body is attempting to communicate.

Your body craves reassurance in distress, and when you don't have access to your spouse's reassurance, you can receive a kind, tender, soothing response from yourself.

Ask yourself, *What's happening? Does something seem familiar? What might be familiar?*

As you remember, you can also offer words of reassurance to yourself:

Of course that was overwhelming for me.
Of course that stung.
Of course I felt panicked in that moment.

You can name these feelings and offer yourself validation and comfort.

Reassurance can also help you attune to what you're experiencing and what you need in the moment. Remember when we said earlier that removing judgment can help us see more of what is really going on? This is true not only toward our partner but also toward ourselves. When we observe ourselves without any judgment, we can respond and tend to ourselves better. We find true answers when we say, *I wonder what would be helpful* or *I wonder what my body needs.*

The practice of attunement to your own body develops muscle memory. This not only gives you access to what you need but also equips you to disrupt reenactments with your spouse. You replace old messages about yourself and about perceived threats from your spouse with the present reality of safety, care, compassion, and kindness.

In these moments keep in mind how powerful the change agents of humility and honesty are. Humility opens up your ability to be aware and attune to what is happening in you and your spouse and to disrupt the triggering of trauma, both past and present. Honesty reveals your hurts and failures, your wounds and tender places, and allows you to own what is yours without blaming your spouse or others.

Look for moments today when you can practice more of this gentleness toward frailty, grace toward failure, and openness to change. Answer the following questions right now and keep them in mind as a way of grounding yourself and self-attuning whenever you experience a sense of being triggered or dysregulated.

- How do I habitually protect and defend myself? What past harm and trauma contribute to these reactive habits and patterns?
- What are the explanations and justifications I repeatedly come back to? How have I used these to protect myself in the past? And how do they impede intimacy with my spouse in the present?
- What past harm might my body be remembering in moments of conflict with my spouse? How does this manifest physically? Where and how do I feel this in my body?
- When my body remembers something familiar, how do I use judgment to perpetuate the cycle? How can I respond in a way that acknowledges and cares for my body instead?

Part 5

Creating New Patterns

S ustained awareness.

This lifelong practice is the foundational task to create new patterns of intimate inter-action with your spouse. Becoming more aware—of yourself and your spouse—is a lifetime process that requires a willingness to honor what you know, be intrigued, and be open to what you are still unaware of. Human beings are gifted with neuroplasticity in our brains, meaning we can form new neural pathways that lead to new thinking, feeling, and behaviors and even more to new joy. The work ahead is to grow in awareness and create new patterns and establish new neural pathways by practicing new patterns.

Awareness is not a performance level or skill that you can master and be done. Sustained awareness requires trial-and-error practices to re-form our brains, let alone our way of being in the world. At first, new patterns will feel awkward, if not insincere—even when we know and want to be different. Persisting through those moments will allow us to address the many forces—seen and unseen—at war with change.

Part 5 invites you to take your seeds of awareness and cultivate new sustainable patterns. While this process is organic, it is also progressive, which means it is helpful to go step-by-step and develop the skills consistent with your current level before trying to ascend to the next tier. Of course, there will be overlap, but taking smaller steps consistently rather than trying to make huge jumps tends to create more lasting change.

Here are some big ideas we will explore in Part 5:

- Creating new patterns requires humility, honesty, kindness, grief, and defiant hope.
- Humility is simply removing the log in one's own eye before addressing the speck in another's.
- Honesty sweeps aside excuses, justifications, and defenses once you've named the log. Honesty opens the door to a conversation on its context and impact.
- Kindness embodies a fierce commitment to entering your spouse's heartache and fear with compassion and care. It also expresses righteous anger at past harm.
- Grief laments the harm we have endured, the harm our spouses have suffered, and the harm we have caused one another. Grief enables us to ask for and offer comfort.
- Defiant hope stands against distraction, discouragement, and despair and practices attentiveness, diligence, and perseverance in order for your marriage to grow.

5.1

How Can You Replace
Old Patterns with New Ones?

Our work in marriage is not simply to resolve conflict but to integrate
fruitful ways to stay connected to each other throughout it.

THE DEEP-ROOTED MARRIAGE, P. 153

Change is the only constant.

You have likely heard this irrefutable paradox many times. Some people seem to thrive on change and enjoy the dynamic energy it brings. Others resist change at all costs and prefer to stick with what's familiar, even when change offers new and better options. Most of us fall somewhere between the extremes, reluctant to change in some areas of our lives and eager to move forward in others.

When it comes to growing deeper roots in your marriage, you will experience this tension repeatedly. You, along with your spouse, want to see change in how you relate to each other, to dispel certain dynamics and eradicate old scripts and replace them with more effective responses and intimate vulnerability. Facilitating such change, however, requires a commitment to ongoing practices that may seem uncomfortable, awkward, or uncertain at first.

You may feel triggered by risking vulnerability yet again with the one person who knows best where you are tender and raw. Your old default responses have been in place for decades, and replacing them will likely be an ongoing endeavor throughout the rest of your lives together. This replacement process may not bring the immediate results you long to experience, but quick fixes rarely do more than irritate deep wounds. Even when behaviors change, if underlying causal issues from past traumas are not addressed, such attempts falter.

You and your partner committed to a shared life together through adversity and prosperity, good times and hard seasons, richer and poorer, sickness and health. Your marriage involves doing life together, and if you want to move beyond symptomatic conflicts and persistent impasses, then improving your relationship calls for patience in the process. It requires diligence in what you've been discovering and exploring in your own story as well as your spouse's story.

Replacing old patterns with new ones means having an ongoing commitment to practice humility (extend grace not judgment) and honesty (essential for change to endure), to grieve (both individually and jointly), to defy the obstacles (past and present), and to bless one another (fully and generously). Once again, the goal is not to eliminate conflict, tension, and disagreement but to sustain connection and experience intimacy in the midst of what you encounter. In order for your marriage to grow deeper roots, perseverance not perfection is required.

Yes, change is the only constant.

Harnessing change in your marriage, however, takes practice.

- Do you consider yourself someone who usually embraces and adapts to change quickly or a person who resists change in favor of the familiar? What about your spouse?
- What are some of the "quick fixes" you and your partner have used previously in hopes of improving your relationship? What did you learn from trying them?

Breaking the Surface

If you have ever renovated or remodeled a home, you know the process requires discernment, vision, patience, and perseverance. Before the actual work begins, you must assess what to keep and what to eliminate as you preserve the "good bones" of the structure and remove the outdated and dysfunctional features. Once these decisions have been made, you can proceed to the demolition phase, knocking down walls to create new spaces and updating electrical and plumbing systems.

Beginning to replace old relational patterns in your marriage with new ones also requires a process of assessment and demolition. As you become more aware of the walls and barriers erected, you each can take ownership and share the responsibility of removing them in order to create new space together. Your initial tool for this process is humility.

Simply put, humility acknowledges the log in your own eye before addressing the speck in your spouse's. Practicing humility as the foundation for replacing old patterns with new ones first requires that you pause, own the hurt, name the log in your own eye, and invite interaction with your spouse. Rather than defending yourself, pouring contempt, and shifting blame, you discover humility creates space for intimacy in the midst of tension.

Depending on the context, practicing humility may lead you to acknowledge, "I am wrong; forgive me." If those words feel true, say them. Owning the log in your own eye gives you a chance to begin a conversation that can take you to a deeper understanding of yourself and what your spouse felt. This is not the same as jumping to an apology or absorbing blame, which tend to end the conversation rather than opening the door to engage what has just occurred.

When you are hurt and triggered, it is nearly impossible to stop your trauma responses. No one can walk on water or defy gravity, but you can allow awareness to prepare you for immersion into the water. You can learn to sense the range of your responses. As you become more aware of how you typically respond, you can help your spouse learn to spot them as well.

Writing out and diagramming a recent conflict or triggering incident with your spouse can be a fruitful exercise for you both. Similar to Nourishing the Roots in Part 4, this process allows you to recognize what needs adjusting and how you might go about making different choices. When you chart the old choreography in your usual dance of harm, you can then change the rhythm, tempo, and steps taken to move toward alignment. Let me (Dan) give you an example based on the scenario I described previously:

Becky: Oh, I wouldn't use that olive oil if you are going to make a stir-fry.

My wife's initial volley is meant to be helpful. But it fails to engage the reality that the kitchen has been a battleground for us for a while. Without an acknowledgment of prior struggles and their scaffolding, you overlook your spouse's story as well as your own.

Dan: I have used olive oil a hundred times. What's the big deal with the way I'm doing it?

My response to her "help" is defensive and challenging by using hyperbole and an angry tone to make her pay for offering her counsel. My question appears rhetorical but is, in fact, accusatory and judgmental. Implicit are bigger, uglier questions: "Do you always have to criticize me? You just cannot let anything go, can you?"

Becky: Olive oil doesn't hold heat as well as saffron.

Instead of addressing my defensive tone, her straightforward, logical answer attempts to cover the tension and pretend there is no conflict. This is a good example of using a left-brain cognitive process to resolve a right-brain defensive response. It never works. We have to engage right-brain to right-brain.

Dan: Whatever. If you want to do the stir-fry, you can do it your way.

Notice how my other-centered contempt increases and threatens to disrupt dinner and, in turn, cut off the relationship. I make it clear that I am about to withdraw.

Becky: Why are you angry? You don't need to be mean.

Other-centered contempt is then countered by hurt-fueled blame. Such hurt-fueled questions are seldom invitations to explore or understand. Instead, the question implies judgment followed by the accurate but defensive accusation of meanness.

Dan: No matter what I do in your kitchen, it always needs to be corrected.

Instead of increasing an other-centered attack, the tone changes to a hurt-fueled, self-pitying, self-contemptuous withdrawal that serves as an indirect attack. This specific incident becomes generalized to reflect our usual dance steps.

Becky: Just stop it. I am not even hungry. Do whatever you want.

Other-centered contempt comes fully to the surface, along with the accusation that you have ruined my dinner, and there is stonewalling to cut off more hurt.

Both: [Silence and withdrawal.]

It took awhile for us to pen out this dialogue. We both felt shame, hurt, and anger. We could have ignored it, forgiven each other, and moved on. But we would not have recognized the themes that play out often in our conflicts. The dance has variations and complexity, but the steps are often repetitive and recognizable: Becky is helpful. I feel humiliated. I get angry. She becomes logical and reasonable. I up the ante and become judgmental and harsh. She lashes back and shuts down. We both quit.

We will come back to this scene and consider other responses momentarily. But now it's your turn to take a recent exchange and look at the pattern. Use the following questions to help you pay attention to the way you each go back and forth in this dance.

- What was the initial volley, the comment or action, that caused the interaction to begin? How did it trigger you or your spouse?
- What defensive responses were activated and displayed? How did this ignite a back-and-forth dance of any of the following: retaliation, judgment, contempt, or withdrawal?
- Looking at what was spoken, how did your words convey so much more than their surface meaning? What unspoken messages were traded back and forth?
- How would you summarize the recognizable and repetitive dance on display in this exchange? What do you notice about the way you interact within this dance?

Letting In the Light

Exercising humility begins with ongoing awareness. Like any habitual process, the more frequently and consistently you notice what's taking place, the greater your awareness to spot it sooner the next time. And the quicker you can recognize what's taking place between you, the greater the opportunity to create new patterns.

Humility in your marriage begins with awareness and is fostered by pausing, then engaging. Pausing as soon as you become aware of being triggered breaks the usual default sequence of defensive responses. Handling triggers well in the moment takes time and intentional effort. It takes time to lower one's stress biochemicals and come back to one's senses.

If you attempt to "resolve" or "deal with" the issue right away, it will usually escalate into your usual dark dance.

- What keeps you from pausing when one of you is triggered?
- Can you write out an agreement about pausing when one or both are triggered?
- What is your plan for the five minutes (or whatever length of time agreed upon) you need to restore connection?

Once you pause, you can engage what is being triggered. This step requires reengaging your prior work—what you've learned from exploring your stories and past traumas. Triggers reflect keen sensitivity and usually involve overreaction. Simply naming what you're feeling ("I feel humiliated" or "I feel ashamed") is a good beginning.

But of course, there is more. Often, as a child, I (Dan) felt like there was nothing I could do to make my mom feel better. So when I told Becky that I was never able to do anything right in "her" kitchen, it felt true despite being a false overgeneralization. In the middle of the interaction, it felt truer than true. What was required was sufficient distance and pause to make the first move necessary for honor and goodness: displaying humility.

Pausing and engaging allows you to own the hurt. There is no greater humility than admitting you feel hurt at first. Own it. Allow yourself to feel vulnerable—similar to your younger self in moments that somehow resonate similarly—and reactive. This move allows you to acknowledge, "I feel some degree of fragmentation." This is the past and present colliding. What you are feeling may not be called trauma, but you are likely feeling ramped up and ready to fight, flee, freeze, or fawn.

- Where do you feel the hurt in your body? How young and vulnerable do you feel?
- What is your typical response that you want to disrupt? What are the themes in the fight/conflict that resonate with your childhood stories?
- What do I need to own about my trauma response with my spouse? How can I disrupt my usual go-to defensive posture and attitude?

Try writing out your trauma response even if it feels awkward and mechanical. Here's what I wrote Becky to allow us to begin a new conversation: "Becky, I know I overreacted to your suggestion. I used anger and self-pity blended with sarcasm to make you pay. I am aware of how often I am triggered by what I perceive to be a comment that brings humiliation. I am not blaming you. Let's talk."

Living Water

Humility—owning the log in your own eye—is meant to be bound to honesty. More than a willingness to disclose the whole truth, honesty united with humility sweeps aside your excuses, justifications, and defenses. Honesty transcends transparency to include vulnerability. To help clarify further, let's consider what honesty is not:

- Telling the other person where he or she is wrong or failed you
- Justifying or explaining why you failed
- Offering an excuse for your interaction
- Dumping emotional debris on your spouse
- Making light of what occurred

Honesty allows you to begin to explore and make sense of the triggered response. Notice again, this is not a means to make light of what happened or blame-shift the failure to someone else. The trigger is yours—it is the log in your eye. So begin by reflecting on what the log is and how it came to be. You have already done a lot of this work. Now it is being used to further a mutually intimate conversation in the here and now, in real time.

Once you have named the log in your eye, open the door to this kind of conversation by considering its context and impact. Our triggers have a root system that is often far deeper than we understand. It is not enough to cut them off at the surface—merely apologize and move on. Old roots need to be dug up for healthier ones to grow, and it is easy to want to pull the weeds and hope all the unhealthy roots get extracted. Seldom is this the case. Digging in the dirt—getting dirty, messy, and sweaty—is necessary.

The dirty work required for deeper roots in your marriage relies on humility and honesty digging in tandem. This kind of self-awareness and other-consideration comes from owning your own heap before piling onto your spouse's. We see this in Jesus' explanation about removing the log in your own eye before pointing out the speck in someone else's. Read the more contemporary rendering of this passage below and then answer the questions that follow.

> Don't pick on people, jump on their failures, criticize their faults—unless, of course, you want the same treatment. That critical spirit has a way of boomeranging. It's easy to see a smudge on your neighbor's face and be oblivious to the ugly sneer on your own. Do you have the nerve to say, "Let me wash your face for you," when your own face is distorted by contempt? It's this whole traveling road-show mentality all over again, playing a holier-than-thou part instead of just living your part. Wipe that ugly sneer off your own face, and you might be fit to offer a washcloth to your neighbor.
>
> MATTHEW 7:1–5 MSG

- Why are both humility and honesty required in order to disrupt old patterns and default defenses? How does humbly telling the truth to one another differ from the way you used to think about honesty?
- How does considering the context and impact of your defensive responses create opportunity for conversation rather than escalation?
- When have you used the kind of critical spirit Jesus referenced to attack your spouse? How does such criticism fail to use honesty for constructive purposes?
- As you reflect on a recent conflict or triggering incident with your spouse, how did you experience your critical spirit boomeranging?
- What's currently the most challenging aspect of doing the dirty work required to grow deeper roots? What causes you to feel uncomfortable, awkward, anxious, or vulnerable?

Sharing Fruit

Humility and honesty also cultivate empathy. We grow to understand and grow in empathy to the degree we can enter the stories of harm that our spouses have endured. The hurt we are feeling today has its roots in countless early experiences when we were young. Recognizing our own hurt, hitting pause, and then exercising humility and honesty allow us to see the tangled roots of old patterns.

Let's consider an example. A husband often reacted to his wife's hurt by making a quick apology and doing more around the house to please her. She felt frustrated with his quick effort to resolve her hurt and questioned his sincerity and commitment. He then felt judged and confused. He apologized more, and she felt even more dismissed.

Honesty required him to address his relationship with his mother, who was fragile and quick to shut down if he didn't take full responsibility for her tears. Honesty required his wife to name that she grew up in a family that spent many exhausting hours rehashing emotional conflicts, and anything less felt like a lack of love.

What is being named for each is a great beginning, but it isn't enough. Themes have been identified but not in full context of their stories. Curiously enough, we often don't remember significant stories to share. But if we begin with what we know, more details and depth often return in the telling and even more in the retelling.

We may also be reluctant to share our stories because we often don't trust our spouses yet to handle our most significant and painful ones. Your trust will grow as you take time to engage what is less difficult and move to share what is more complex. Be careful not to judge your spouse's response to what you share. There is a beginning to all root growth. His or her response is likely not fully what you desire, but take in what is experienced and know you are developing a new root system.

A story told is a story meant to be retold many more times. It is like excavation. In an archaeological dig, you find a shard of a pot. One doesn't stop there and assume there is nothing more. One significant finding requires that the digging get slower and more methodical. You will learn to assume there is always more to find. Plan to come back to the story, or if new elements or stories feel connected, then open the door to where the new elements or stories take you.

Also, keep in mind that it's easy to tell or hear the story without letting yourself *feel* what is happening, particularly with repetition in sharing a particular story. It is part of trauma to feel and remain numb. We can tell stories like a reporter going through the facts of a crime without letting ourselves feel. And if the feelings simply are not there, consider what is keeping you from feeling more. Often, identifying and expressing the blockage opens the door for us to feel more.

5 . 2

What Are Some New Responses
You Can Practice?

*We all are bent toward blaming each other, and our bias blinds
us to key aspects of reality. Even when we have been wronged, we
need to take whatever is blinding us out of our eyes first.*

THE DEEP-ROOTED MARRIAGE, P. 160

If you have ever seen an example of *kintsugi*, the centuries-old Japanese artistic tradition of repairing broken pottery to new glory, then you know the stunning result. The method is based on a profound Japanese philosophy that brokenness can be tended to and made beautiful. It is the reversal of all that seems sensible. How can shards not only be brought back together but made stronger and more beautiful? Gold lacquer, rather than clear glue, highlights the breaks and fractures while unifying them to new wholeness.

Repair in your marriage will similarly defy logic and reasoning to create new beauty. It will feel both astounding and risky, especially as you give your partner access to your wounds and stories. But you are meant to be seen and known, to be honored and cared for, and you can choose to invite the deepest experiences of these things into your marriage. There will be countless conflicts and ruptures for you to navigate, but as you grow stronger together over time, the duration of your disconnection will lessen, and you'll find ways to cultivate intimacy amid tension.

Opening your heart to your partner is a courageous act that begins this process of mending what is broken. It shifts your loyalty from disconnection to connection and tells your spouse, *I choose you, and I choose us.* Such bold love depicts the mind-boggling claim of the resurrection— that death doesn't get the final word, all losses will be redeemed, and even the scars of the cross will reflect the glory of God.

This is the bigger story of restoration that your marriage story gets to reflect.

If you can approach your spouse not with the intent to blame or judge or harm but with gifts of curiosity and kindness, compassion and safety, then your defiance resurrects new life in your relationship. Despite both your failures, even with all the broken promises and sharp-edged interactions, you can experience a beautiful new wholeness.

- Search for images of kintsugi on your phone or device and consider how the broken pieces have been reunited to form a new whole. What stands out or resonates most with you as you compare your marriage to this extraordinary art form?
- What old grudges, mistakes, failures, and betrayals continue to linger in the background of your relationship with your spouse? How can these be welcomed and addressed into creating new life in your marriage?

Breaking the Surface

More than twenty years ago, scientists discovered what they called *mirror neurons* in monkeys being studied. Further study revealed that these unique neurons also are present in humans and provide the neural foundation for empathy, giving us the capacity to sense others' emotions and mirror them.

When someone smiles, we are apt to smile as well. If they clench their jaws in anger, we're likely to do the same. When newborns hear another baby crying, they orient their bodies toward the sound. Humans feel what other humans feel; we respond to others' distress with our own distress.

This phenomenon applies to your marriage as well. Researchers have also found that entering the suffering of our spouses builds intimacy and marital satisfaction. This finding correlates with the neuroscience truism that "what fires together, wires together."

What deepens your emotional attunement increases your relational intimacy.

Simply put, if you don't suffer for your spouse, you will not grow the roots of your love. Plenty of obstacles stand in your way, of course. None of us are naturally inclined to choose suffering. You may honestly feel unable to bear even your own suffering; how could you possibly take on more? In fact, a tragic result of your trauma is that you've learned to shut down your emotional attunement to your own suffering, which also dulls your capacity to feel on behalf of others. It's no surprise, then, that you're probably reluctant to engage with your spouse's struggles when you have little practice with your own.

Consider how you and your spouse handle illness, for example. Illness keeps us from functioning at our typical level. We can't escape needing care, which can be an intolerable reality. Many of us with histories of significant trauma want to push through illness, avoid rest, and pretend we don't need help. We resent care when it reminds us that we are weak.

But we are meant to suffer each other's frailties and the stories that have turned our hearts against needing help. Looking at the past can inform the future, shaping the way we handle friction and suffer together in the days to come.

If you want to write a new marriage story, this different pattern of goodness, strength, and togetherness is what you want to establish.

- When have you experienced the effect of mirror neurons and found yourself taking on the mood, feelings, or expression of your spouse? When have you noticed your partner taking on yours?
- Based on your experience, do you agree that emotional attunement increases relational intimacy? Why or why not?
- How do you usually respond when battling a cold, the flu, or another short-term illness? How does your response differ from your spouse's when he or she is sick?
- What have you learned from your spouse about feeling empathy for others? What has your spouse learned from you?
- Who struggles most with being needy and requiring care from the other—you or your spouse? How are you each learning to adjust to expressing needs and receiving help?

Letting In the Light

Empathy paves the way to lament the harm you have endured, the trauma your spouse has suffered, and the pain you have caused each other. The more you know, the more you may feel compelled to weep. Suffering softens your hearts toward one another as you grieve past losses.

It is one thing to hear that a terrible accident has taken the lives of a hundred people in a plane crash. Most human beings feel something like sadness or grief at such news. It is an entirely different level of grief when we hear about some of the people on the plane. When we see the faces of a young mother and her two kids, we can't help but wonder what the last few minutes were like for her as she cared for her children as the plane fell out of the sky. If we see her photo with her children and read about her life, the intensity of the loss grows.

Our process of suffering is no different for our spouses.

The closer and deeper we get into our stories of past harm and the stories of our spouses, the more our hearts will suffer. The more curiosity opens us to imagine the suffering of our spouses in greater detail, the more our grief and anger will grow. We experience some of what they have been carrying, validating their pain and releasing it as a solitary burden.

Grief enables us to ask for and offer comfort. Jesus said, "Blessed are those who mourn, for they will be comforted" (Matthew 5:4). Intimacy in our marriages is not fostered primarily by romantic overtures. Our capacity to feel what our spouses have suffered deepens intimacy—whether they are willing or able to do so.

Be aware that the spouse sharing a story is often more defensive and protective of what he or she feels than the spouse hearing the story. We who suffered in our families of origin or through different kinds of abuse have a long and tragic history of shutting down, dismissing, making light of, or ignoring the pain. Seldom will we both come to the same event of harm and feel the same degree of grief or anger.

But there is no need for this disparity in the "felt experience" to drive us to despair. Of course, there will be frustration and confusion, but the more you understand your own reluctance to enter these emotions, the more you can honor how difficult it is for your spouse.

Grief opens our hearts to comfort, which grounds us in attunement. But we need more from our spouses (and ourselves) than grief. We need someone who is a witness to the injustice and harm we endured and feels angry. Anger can deflect, blame, and be used to fuel vengeance. The anger we need is a fist-pounding desire to stand against what happened and work to repair the breach.

Living Water

When we offer our spouses the gifts of grief and anger, we are giving them the gift of kindness—which is not merely a pleasantry to avoid conflict or gain acceptance. Kindness is the fierce commitment to offer goodness to ourselves and others.

We are promised that the kindness of God leads to repentance (Romans 2:4). The promise is that we change (repent, turn, replace old patterns with new ones) through the gift of kindness, not through guilt, pressure, judgment, or contempt. Kindness is not niceness; instead, the intersection of strength (righteous anger) and tenderness (sacred grief) moves toward the heart, reminding us that we are beloved. Kindness is not avoiding conflict or making the other pay during conflict. It is a willingness to bring tenderness to hurt parts and a protective shield of anger to witness and defend the parts that have been harmed.

This kind of divine kindness can also eliminate the demilitarized zones (DMZs) that have developed in your relationship. A DMZ is a well-defined space that forces two sides of a conflict not to traverse. The DMZ between North and South Korea is a no-persons land that, if you enter, will likely result in you being shot by both sides. It is terrain that offers a counterfeit peace—often avoidance—that is no peace.

In a marriage, a DMZ is a recognized area that has brought so much heartache and conflict that it is not worth the risk of taking a walk into the danger. These are the hot spots that have repeatedly proved to be land mines of contempt, judgment, criticism, and withdrawal. But here is the dilemma: The more we avoid a tough issue, the bigger it grows. Not only because we are operating out of fear but also because evil uses this languid land to plant seeds of resentment that eventually grow into various forms of hatred.

Untended resentment will grow into a judgment of contempt that eventually will kill a marriage, even if the two partners don't divorce. Some intact marriages are sustained only by the mutual enjoyment of resenting each other. It is a travesty of God's design that instead of love bonding us, hatred serves the same purpose.

This is why emotional attunement and a willingness to suffer for one another are vital to dispelling DMZs and creating new safe spaces. As you know, suffering for anyone, even ourselves and our spouses, often feels counterintuitive and triggers the old defenses that once helped us survive. But the results of intimacy, love, honor, and delight are more than worth it. This paradox emerges in the teachings of Jesus known as the Beatitudes, a series of blessings basically resulting from suffering. Read them below and then answer the questions that follow.

You're blessed when you're at the end of your rope. With less of you there is more of God and his rule.

You're blessed when you feel you've lost what is most dear to you. Only then can you be embraced by the One most dear to you.

You're blessed when you're content with just who you are—no more, no less. That's the moment you find yourselves proud owners of everything that can't be bought.

You're blessed when you've worked up a good appetite for God. He's food and drink in the best meal you'll ever eat.

You're blessed when you care. At the moment of being "care-full," you find yourselves cared for.

You're blessed when you get your inside world—your mind and heart—put right. Then you can see God in the outside world.

You're blessed when you can show people how to cooperate instead of compete or fight. That's when you discover who you really are, and your place in God's family.

MATTHEW 5:3–9 MSG

- What does it mean to be kind to yourself as you face your spouse's failures? What does it look like to show kindness to your spouse when he or she fails you?
- When do you tend to prefer contempt over kindness in the midst of conflict with your spouse? What's required for you to put contempt aside and choose to offer kindness?
- What are some of the DMZs in your marriage? How do they reflect the core of old patterns that are no longer needed?
- What stands out to you in the Beatitudes? What are you willing to suffer in order to experience blessing in your marriage?

Consider asking God to reveal his kindness to you as you engage these questions. As you do, what do you find your heart moving toward?

Sharing Fruit

Growing a marriage, like any plant, requires attentiveness and diligence. Consistent growth requires perseverance. The process is phenomenally rewarding, like tending to a fruit tree that, year by year, offers sweet-tasting fruit, but it doesn't happen without intention. Sustainable growth requires the tenacity of defiant hope.

Defiant hope is not mere optimism or a positive view of the future. This hope defies the odds and, at times, logic as it remains willing to risk and endure the inevitable ups and downs of your marriage. Such hope is not a fantasy; it is a hardfisted dream that we are willing to bleed and suffer for in order to see it come about.

Exercising defiant hope requires dealing with distractions, disappointment, and despair. The first category here, distractions, comes in many forms. Distractions can take your focus, consume your passion, and stall your progress. There's nothing wrong with playing pickleball or computer games, nor is it wrong to watch favorite shows or check out Instagram. But we all know we can lose hours by following every news story, clicking on every link, or golfing every weekend.

There are personal and relational benefits to hiking, exploring, playing, and cultivating joy in anything from knitting to skydiving. But are we staying aware of the ways distractions shift our focus? We can find more relief from stress in our distractions than courage to deal with the stress head-on. We can find more pleasure from our distractions than we do in dealing with the ups and downs in our marriages. When our chosen distractions become our preferred escapes from reality, then they have become a god. Defiant hope refuses to let distractions pull time, energy, attention, and resources away from what matters most—your relationship with your beloved.

Like distractions, disappointment—in ourselves and in our spouses—is inevitable. We desire, and our desires are often not met. When our desires and dreams underperform, we can feel the sigh of disappointment. Disappointment, however, is not the issue—the trap is resentment. Repeated disappointment sets our hearts up for sickness (Proverbs 13:12).

No matter how deep the disappointment, turning away from your spouse and closing him or her out of your heart is turning away from God as well. It is understandable; it is not acceptable.

Defiant hope fuels the difficult and demanding commitment to address how resentment has become like plaque in your heart. Over countless years, the resentment has become a trusted friend and protector—but it is a liar and a fraud. It appears to serve you well even as it hurts you.

Resentment eventually wears you down and undermines your marriage. Unaddressed resentment, like untreated cancer, will take your life. Defiant hope keeps disappointment tempered so that it cannot solidify into brittle resentment.

Unchecked, resentment usually evolves into despair. You may believe your marriage is beyond hope, that lasting change is simply not possible. Once such resignation becomes an acceptable conclusion, the challenge to resurrect your relationship becomes not impossible but certainly more formidable. Defiant hope stops planning for the end and refuses to focus on a new beginning until the present has been addressed and engaged.

Nourishing the Roots

Whether or not we're conscious of it, we all long to see beauty grow out
of ashes. This is exactly what practicing repair ultimately produces.
We experience restoration. We learn to build trust and deepen
intimacy. To expand the care we offer each other. To stand against
the trauma our beloved has suffered and pursue healing.

THE DEEP-ROOTED MARRIAGE, P. 164

As you consider how to replace old harmful patterns with new life-giving responses, you may grow weary and experience moments of discouragement. This is to be expected. The process, however, requires a long-term commitment to repair the ruptures in your marriage by doing the work necessary to grow deeper relational roots together. This commitment can remind you of the work you each are doing as well as the shared endeavor of pursuing new levels of intimacy.

By now you know that this Nourishing the Roots section is intended to help sustain your progress toward growth in more personal ways. It's to be completed by you along with your spouse, if possible, rather than as part of a group study. As before, you can decide whether to share your experience with your group at your next meeting. But focus on completing it here for the exclusive benefit of you and your spouse and your relationship.

This exercise once again invites you to draw on all the hard work and improved awareness you have been cultivating. The goal here is to think through and reflect on the good gifts you can continue bestowing on your spouse as well as receive from him or her. You will be asked to consider your best motives, possible obstacles, and potential outcomes from these gifts. Finally, you will be encouraged to consider concrete ways to put these gifts into tangible practice in your daily interactions.

The Gift of Curiosity

You have likely experienced conversations in which the other person monopolized your discussion. Depending on the context and depth of your relationship, you may not have realized your interaction revolved around that person's life, family, career, interests, and accomplishments. Or you may have endured the self-absorbed monologue out of politeness or a reluctance to fight for airtime. Regardless, these conversations usually remain one-sided because of a lack of self-awareness as well as a deficiency in curiosity by the nonstop speaker.

Curiosity may come more naturally to some people than others, but it can be cultivated by intentional inquiry as you practice pausing when aware of being triggered. So often we have become conditioned to jump to conclusions as quickly as possible, assessing and analyzing, embracing or distancing, recognizing or resisting whatever we might be experiencing. We are inherently hardwired to avoid pain, danger, and discomfort in order to ensure our bodies' survival. But as we have seen, we can get stuck in old neural pathways that once protected us but are no longer needed.

So rather than allowing default responses of shame, contempt, judgment, and condemnation to persist, you can cultivate curiosity for yourself and your spouse. Practicing curiosity with your own feelings, thoughts, and responses enables you to continue making connections between past traumas and present reactions. You can pause and ask yourself what it is you're feeling and experiencing, where you feel it in your body, and why you might be feeling it at that moment in that particular context.

This same process of inquiry can also become a gift given to your spouse. Curiosity compels the intentional entering of his or her story and experience, which further develops and reinforces a desire to know and understand what your spouse feels, desires, and fears. Expressing sincere curiosity shows your willingness to relinquish attention on yourself and to engage him or her.

Expressing curiosity about what our spouses are experiencing, how it's manifesting, and why it may have been triggered results in deeper attunement and intimate alignment. As we listen and focus on their responses, we may then ask gentle follow-up questions, mirroring and validating our understanding of them. Our focused engagement indicates our commitment to know them fully, accepting them regardless of how they may feel and loving them in the midst of emotional messiness.

- How often do you ask questions about your spouse that go beyond details of the day, or what happened, or what needs to be done to plan an event? Can you give an example?
- What would you like to know about your spouse's life, past, present, or future that you have not asked?
- What has kept you from asking? What do you fear might occur if you were to ask?
- What areas, experiences, thoughts, or feelings do you wish your spouse would explore in you? How can you convey this without asking directly?

Gift-in-Action: For the next week, look for organic opportunities to exercise curiosity with your spouse each day. Try not to make it obvious in a way that feels contrived or insincere and, instead, shift your attitude to one of being open-minded and open-hearted toward your partner. This may require you to let go of past conclusions and previous expectations about how you assume your spouse feels and thinks in the moment. Create room for curious questioning for the sake of making new discoveries.

The Gift of Kindness

Once again, it's vitally important to distinguish between genuine kindness and simply being nice, polite, or deferential. You will recall that niceness is often strategic pleasantry used to avoid conflict and pain or to manipulate others into acceptance. Kindness, by contrast, chooses to offer goodness boldly by exercising humility and honesty. Kindness embodies a fierce commitment to enter the heartache and fear of your spouse with compassion and care.

The gift of kindness is motivated by repentance and restoration, by redemption and reconciliation. Your kindness results from the kindness of God, from the gift of his grace rather than judgment and condemnation. The apostle Paul reminded the Romans that refusing God's gift of kindness keeps us trapped in contempt—for ourselves and for others: "Do you show contempt for the riches of his kindness, forbearance and patience, not realizing that God's kindness is intended to lead you to repentance?" (Romans 2:4).

Kindness is the choice not to rush the process but to take time to understand how the harm occurred and where you find yourselves now. Sorting through the shards of past harm bonds you together in shared grief, giving you a clearer perspective of your story and setting you up for restoration. Kindness does not manipulate or shift from the present moment; kindness bears the weight of whatever your spouse feels, recalls, and suffers from past trauma and harm.

Exercising kindness relies on an attitude of humility and commitment to honesty. Kind humility is your ability to be attuned and aware of what is happening in yourself and in your spouse in order to disrupt the triggering of trauma, both past and present. Kind honesty takes ownership of what is felt without blaming your partner's actual or perceived failure. It addresses the log in your own eye rather than shifting focus to your spouse's speck. The gift of kindness reflects all the qualities of love described in 1 Corinthians 13 and puts them into action.

- How has your spouse shown you kindness in the midst of your trauma responses and triggering incidents? How does that kindness provide insight as to how you can show kindness to him or her?
- When have you used niceness rather than kindness to avoid conflict or gloss over a painful subject or persistent issue? What would a kind response look like instead?
- What has motivated your past attempts at kindness toward your partner? How do you hope the way you show kindness will be different moving forward?
- How can you continue to use humility and honesty to facilitate the gift of kindness in your marriage? What might this look like the next time your spouse is triggered?

Gift-in-Action: As you consider all you know about your spouse's story, think about how you can show a willingness to sustain your curiosity and empathy in his or her suffering. This might be as simple as choosing not to return the focus to your own experience but to remain engaged as you actively listen, allowing for silence and sharing space with your spouse even if it is uncomfortable or painful. Or it might be taking action to help him or her face the impact of past trauma by reading or watching a relevant resource together, discussing and following up in couple's counseling, or pursuing a retreat devoted to healing and recovery. Don't think too long, though, before choosing to do something—at the very least, begin a conversation in which you inquire about what your spouse needs and wants from you.

The Gift of Suffering

The gift of kindness opens your heart to extend the gift of suffering, a willingness to experience anger and grief on behalf of your spouse. Particularly as you enter his or her story and hear about incidents of harm, neglect, and abuse, your response reflects your willingness to suffer at least a taste of what your spouse has suffered and continues to endure. The closer and deeper you go into your beloved's suffering, the more you will hurt with him or her. Out of your hurt, anger and grief emerge.

In the midst of learning about both past and present harm done to your spouse, you may feel overwhelmed and hesitant about how to respond. You want to provide what he or she needs but also realize that nothing you do or say can compensate or change the impact of the past. In those moments, remember that your spouse is aware of this as well and does not expect you to take away his or her pain—but dares to hope you will share it.

Anger and grief demonstrate the indignation and sadness you feel in the wake of your spouse's pain. You have the privilege of being a witness to past incidents in ways no one was present to acknowledge at the time those soul injuries were inflicted. Your willingness to remain curious, to ask and receive painful details of your spouse's story, reflects your desire to come alongside him or her. Your choice to suffer gifts your spouse with an awareness that he or she no longer has to remain alone or isolated in pain.

The gift of suffering draws on other gifts to attune as closely as possible to your beloved.

- How has your heart suffered as you have gotten closer to your spouse's story? When you see the young person who was harmed, what words do you want to offer your spouse?
- If you could show up as an adult at the moment of your spouse's harm, what would you say and do to protect him or her?
- Is it easier to feel grief or anger as you enter the scene of his or her harm? How does your answer reflect your own past harm?

- What would you say and do if you, as an adult, could show up at the moment of your own harm as a child or adolescent?

Gift-in-Action: This gift may seem more challenging to extend but remains essential to growing deeper roots in your marriage. And suffering for and with your spouse is not a switch that can be flipped on and off. Instead, it is an ongoing awareness and subsequent sensitivity to all that has harmed him or her in the past. Drawing on your current awareness and attunement to your partner, choose and share an image, artwork, song, photo, or other creative expression that you believe resonates and conveys some aspect of the impact of his or her past trauma. Like a kintsugi bowl with its broken shards restored by veins of gold, your item should reflect the way beauty can emerge from the ashes, a new wholeness from what has been shattered.

The Gift of Defiant Hope

The gift of defiant hope refuses to remain stuck in old patterns and also refuses to let those patterns go unacknowledged and unexamined. Defiant hope knows that the way forward necessitates connecting the past to the present before setting forth to the future. This hope is not a passive, wait-and-see-what-happens kind of wistful hope. Defiant hope is active and vigilant, addressing the distractions, disappointment, and despair that can derail your growth.

Defiant hope moves us to act now rather than wait for change to happen on its own. A proverb tells us: "Hope deferred makes the heart sick" (Proverbs 13:12). Sickness of heart is a form of trauma that fragments, numbs, and isolates. When repeated failures go unaddressed, it is easy to feel hopeless and sick.

Deferred hope cannot sustain the new responses you are now implementing. Postponing the hard, messy work of growing deeper roots will not make the work any easier or less painful. It is common to lose heart by hardening your heart to more deferred hope. As understandable as it is to defend against and depart from hope, it is also a heart-wrenching loss of your humanity. It doesn't just harm whatever might be grown in your marriage; it serves to make you less human and more susceptible to false gods, addictions, affairs, and distractions.

The gift of defiant hope relies on perseverance beyond your human capacities—it relies on sharing a love bigger and more encompassing than what you feel. Defiant hope fertilizes change with the supernatural power of divine love.

- What are the biggest distractions within your control or influence that shift your focus away from your spouse? What would happen if you either gave up or radically cut most of these distractions from your life?
- What's one of your greatest disappointments about your marriage? How have you kept it alive, or even allowed it to harden into resentment, by leaving it unaddressed?
- When have you despaired or allowed yourself to believe that your marriage could not be saved? What has helped prevent your tilt toward despair during challenging times with your spouse?
- What do you need to change in your life in order to exercise defiant hope on a consistent basis? What will help you sustain defiant hope as you face uncertain obstacles ahead?

Gift-in-Action: Shared joy often fuels defiant hope. With this in mind, plan a special date with your spouse that you know will delight him or her. It does not need to be extravagant, but it does need to be exceptional—something you rarely do or haven't done in a long time. Choose something that reflects your attunement to your spouse. It might replicate one of your favorite shared memories from when you were dating or just married, or it might risk something you suspect your spouse has always wanted to experience but never tried. Whether it's an elegant dinner at a new restaurant or a hike to a favorite vista, choose something that will surprise your spouse with a sense of being seen and understood.

Dig deeper with us in the video series using the QR code at the back of the book.

Part 6

Moving Forward

If you have ever hiked, then you know how difficult it can be to assess how much ground you've covered. Depending on the terrain, you might believe you should have reached your summit or campsite hours ago. If you're traversing an icy, muddy trail ascending a Colorado mountain in the spring, you will hike slowly and carefully, minimizing the likelihood of slipping, falling, and injuring yourself. If you're hiking through a well-worn trail during the summer or fall in the rolling hills of the Northeast, you might be surprised by the speed of your progress.

Such adventures usually include facing unexpected obstacles and delays. You may have forgotten a crucial piece of gear, forcing you to return to home base. Your water supply might not have been enough for the heat wave and humidity enveloping you. You may have turned an ankle or discovered your backpack painfully digs into your hips. Nonetheless, you had to figure out how to keep going, moving forward toward your next place of rest and recovery.

As you complete Part 6 of this guidebook, you have similarly covered a lot of ground in pursuit of moving forward. But what are you moving toward? How can any of the hard work and painful digging done by you and your spouse bring you closer together? How can you experience sustainable intimacy? How can you thrive individually as well as together in your attunement of one another? These are the questions to consider as you envision how to take what you know and continue moving forward, nourishing your marriage in ways that ensure deep roots for the rest of your time together.

Here are some big ideas we will explore in Part 6:

- Blessing your spouse fosters intimacy in unique and heavenly ways. Blessing calls out the past, sets the horizon for the future, and honors the person in the present.
- You and your spouse are meant to create goodness together, to bring heaven to earth as you find ways to bless others and honor creation.
- Setting goals for your relationship and creating a regular feedback loop are essential for growing deeper roots in your marriage.
- In the effort to undermine envy and relational opposition and to affirm and nurture your union, recruit and cultivate allies to help you grow your marriage.
- As you set goals and consider what is ahead, you will discover the essential way that play can draw you closer together.

Dig deeper with us in the video series using the QR code at the back of the book.

6 . 1

What Are You Moving Toward?

Every dream is an anticipation of all that awaits us in eternity. Whether
the dream be to fish the South Island of New Zealand one more time
before I die or for my daughter to get the job she has spent months
preparing for—all dreams are when we imagine goodness for ourselves
and others. They are sweet sliver tastes of the banquet ahead.

THE DEEP-ROOTED MARRIAGE, P. 173–174

If you have moved often enough, then you have likely discovered the "10 percent rule." The moment you think you're done, there is still 10 percent left to be done. Often, the 10 percent left to be packed or discarded takes as much time as packing the other 90 percent. At first this realization can be disheartening, and especially due to exhaustion, it often means more gets thrown away and what's left gets tossed randomly into the nearest empty box. You may have discovered items you thought were lost, hidden within the mislabeled box in the garage from the move that occurred years ago.

Tending the deeper roots of your marriage and growing your relationship to produce new, sweeter fruit requires accepting the same ongoing process. While you were enjoying attaining goals and reaching milestones, the work of tending, nurturing, pruning, growing, and harvesting will continue for the rest of your life together. By this point, you are well aware that growing your marriage requires devotion and intentional practices that you share moving forward. The work you have done will be reiterative and grow each time you inquire of one another as well as yourself while facing new trials, struggles, and stories.

Because the process is ongoing, you will do well to create shared goals as part of your growth. We recommend that, at least once a month, you set aside an hour or more to take a walk through an assessment of your marriage. The time should be on the calendar like any other vital appointment and should assess hopes, desires, hindrances, and blessings. You might be surprised by how simply naming and sharing your experiences and their impact on your marriage can be illuminating. Talking about these three areas can also be both preventive and proactive in strengthening your bond.

Realistically, you will face some new challenges that may trigger old ways of responding. When this happens, try to remember that the work you're doing is less about how to solve the problem or manage the crisis and more about how you engage one another to honor and bless rather than to blame and divide. This is meant to be a collaborative process. Resolve what you can, even if it requires significant time, in a way that allows you to bond together.

This intentional process and relational diligence may seem awkward or uncomfortable at first. It may feel impossible to sustain over a lifetime. Once practices are in place and sustained for a significant season, however, the benefits remain even if the practices themselves change or evolve. At regular intervals, perhaps weekly or monthly at first and then every quarter or six months, focus on assessing the changes you're making and the practices that reinforce those changes. Depending on your circumstances and seasons of life, test what works and then revise and revisit as needed. Together, you will discover intentionality and follow-through are more important than the particulars of your plans.

- Have you previously experienced the 10 percent rule when moving? How does it feel to consider that growing deeper roots in your marriage requires an ongoing process as well?
- What do you expect will be one of the greatest challenges you and your spouse will face going forward? What's one goal you can set to address this challenge directly?

Breaking the Surface

If you don't set a goal for your marriage moving forward, then you will have little awareness of whether you're tracking toward the right compass point and going in the direction the two of you have chosen. Usually, the simplest goals are the best. Be careful not to create so many goals that you lose sight of what you are focusing on together. Busy is not the same as focused. Begin with one core issue or theme you both want to address. Some possibilities might include:

- Stopping to pause more quickly and kindly when you are triggered
- Listening more attentively and asking more non-accusatory questions when in conflict
- Walking three mornings each week to connect and sustain connection

Ultimately, the question to ponder is simple: What are the daily/weekly steps you can put in place to achieve your mutually agreed-upon goal(s)? Once in place, simply continue to ask yourselves how you're doing on a regular basis.

Allow your goal setting to be defensive as well as offensive. Addressing obstacles, preferably before they trigger either of you or block your progress, remains a worthy goal toward sustained growth. If you aren't facing obstacles and complications in your marriage, then you are either still on your honeymoon or you are out of touch with reality. At no age is life easy. Challenges and impediments inevitably arise that need to be engaged if you are to grow together. Some possibilities immediately come to mind:

- Time constraints due to unexpected or anticipated new demands
- Financial burdens that require adjustments and concessions
- Health/body disruptions that expose your vulnerability and disrupt your schedules
- Required care for aging parent(s), children, or other loved ones in crisis

At times, merely naming the obstacle allows you to adapt and adjust what is required, not only to deal with the problem but even more so to grow in the process. Once you have identified obstacles, reflect on these questions:

- What would you normally have done in the past due to your unaddressed trauma response? (It is important to set the frame of what might still be a natural/typical response that you don't personally or corporately wish to replicate.)
- What can you do individually and as a couple to experiment with a different response that will bring more goodness to your marriage?

Some obstacles may arise that are insurmountable and overwhelming. Some crises will ultimately be unresolvable. Once again, though, your work is not about answers and solutions but about how to remain connected and attuned in the midst of such disruptive circumstances and unexpected events.

- What, if any, goals have you and your spouse set prior to undertaking the present work you're doing? What contributed to the success or failure of pursuing those goals?
- How do you approach goal setting differently than your spouse? How can you both use these differences to grow closer to one another in pursuit of new goals?
- What's one core issue or theme you both want to address right away? How can you continue to practice new responses rather than default to your old patterns?
- What current obstacles potentially threaten the progress you're making? What's inherent to your current season of life (kids, careers, lifestyle, responsibilities, etc.)?
- What evidence of growth and goodness have you noticed recently in your interactions with your spouse? What's better now than before you began this guidebook?

Letting In the Light

In addition to setting goals and addressing obstacles, the importance of blessing one another cannot be overstated. Blessing is simply growing goodness and bounty in your beloved and in yourself. Nothing is sweeter or more nourishing to your soul than to be blessed. It is so life-changing that you might be apt to trivialize it or even reverse its impact.

You have probably heard the Southern phrase "Bless their heart," which can in fact mean just the opposite, implying contempt, disdain, or pity. To bless someone in this way is basically to curse them.

Perhaps more often the concept of blessing gets trivialized by greeting-card sentimentality and feel-good clichés. This kind of blessing is pithy, predictable, even silly. Cards express sentiments and good wishes for birthdays, anniversaries, graduations, weddings, and even funerals. While these can be sincere expressions of blessing, they usually fall short of blessing that is heartfelt.

Why do most of us struggle with blessing? The answer is simple: we have seldom, if ever, been blessed other than in socially conscripted ways. Perhaps the closest, most personal kind of blessing you've experienced came at your wedding when a parent blessed your union or close friends toasted your new life together. Even these examples, however, can become cloying and unsatisfactory if they are too elaborate, saccharine, or impersonal. We are awkward with blessing because it is too infrequent and too often poorly done, if at all.

True blessing calls out the past and sets the horizon for the future while delighting and honoring the person in the present.

Living Water

A thousand blessings reside in each of us, and much like when a kaleidoscope turns, we continually see the colors in a new configuration. Whether they are spoken or written, blessings are meant over countless reiterations to form a mosaic of such beauty that it takes your breath away each time you experience it. While their impact is intricately layered, the words used are often simple and direct.

We see a paradigm of blessing in the words Jesus used to describe the master's pleasure in the parable of the talents (Matthew 25:14–30). Upon returning home and discovering that those entrusted to steward his resources had profited an increase, the master told them, "Well done, my good and faithful servant" (Matthew 25:23 NLT). This blessing is similar to the words Jesus heard immediately after his baptism by John the Baptist: "This is my beloved Son, with whom I am well pleased" (Matthew 3:17 ESV).

This blessing also awaits those who will one day stand before Jesus: "Welcome, my good and faithful servant!" As brief as they are, the words convey a nearly incomprehensible blessing. Let's consider each word and what it conveys:

Welcome: You are wanted here. You belong. You are home—anticipated, prepared for, and safe.

My: You belong to him. This personal pronoun identifies you as his.

Good: The word echoes God's response at the end of every day of creation: "It is good." The word is also translated "beautiful." Jesus is calling you, his beloved, beautiful.

Faithful: If literal, this word seems untrue. You know how unfaithful you have been. Yet God's sight is to see you through the love of his beloved Son; therefore, you are seen in all that you do and don't do, as faithful as the one who loves you.

Servant: You have followed him and served his purposes no matter how stumbling your steps. Giving someone a cup of cold water has been seen as giving the same to Jesus. Everything you have given away and built for his glory is acknowledged, whether big or small, full of self-interest or not.

- What do you see in your spouse's past that brings you gratitude? Awe?
- What do you envision your spouse doing and becoming in the future that makes you proud?
- What does your spouse do in the present that brings delight?

Look over your responses and add an example to support your answer for each. Now take all those elements and form a blessing. Write it out without stopping to edit or revise—try to let it flow as if you were talking to your spouse. Forget about whether it sounds like a blessing or seems particularly profound or poetic. All beginnings are awkward and require a degree of failure. Even if you both end up giggling over how stilted it sounds, you are at least enjoying this shared blessing. Yours will be unique and quite different, but here is an example that I (Dan) wrote for Becky not long ago:

"Becky, your fierce love and wild, playful heart have brought solace to us when we feel like orphans, and you have dreamt for us to become free to create what we could not have imagined when we first started on this journey together. You saw a way forward that invited God to honor our steps even when we tracked in mud and broke his—and each other's—heart. We remain debtors to his love as we find ways to bring divine presence through our own love to all those we serve. You are beloved, my dearest of all loves."

Now, it's your turn. Don't try to write a Hallmark card or script a monologue from a rom-com. Write it for an audience of one—your beloved in whom you delight and are well pleased.

Sharing Fruit

Blessing is found in deeds as well as words. We bless each time we think about our spouses and bring something into the orbit that offers them a taste of their goodness. We show them that we see them and know their hearts well enough to recognize what brings them joy and delight. Blessings put in action reflect a degree of care and thoughtfulness that goes beyond what is expected in order to transcend this world by offering a momentary taste of heaven. These deeds don't need an occasion and often have greater impact when they emerge in your daily routines. While the possibilities are endless, they might include the following:

- Serving breakfast in bed for no occasion
- Washing the dishes and cleaning up the kitchen
- Planning a well-orchestrated birthday
- Taking the kids to school
- Initiating intimacy
- Making a hard decision that your spouse doesn't want to make
- Saying no to a wonderful but exhausting offer

By now you have some idea of your spouse's love language and the kinds of gifts that are meaningful to him or her. Or if you're still in the process of discovering what your partner enjoys most, acts of blessing allow you wonderful opportunities to explore and discover together. The key is simple: "I am thinking of you and acting to bring you goodness. I don't expect or demand a parade or repayment—my joy is in blessing you."

Two kinds of deeds carry particularly powerful blessings—those that communicate "hell, no!" and "heaven, yes!" The first sets boundaries to prioritize your relationship and protect it from evil. The second unites your hearts as a team to bless others by sharing God's goodness.

Hell, No

There is a profound blessing when we recognize evil and its intent for our destruction and say, "hell, no." The awareness that we are being targeted and endangered and that we need to slam our fists on the table is a profound blessing to our spouses. For example, naming an addiction and taking it on despite the painful, messy process is saying, "hell, no." Choosing to shut down a distraction and naming it as a barrier to the intimacy you're growing and experiencing together is a blessing. It says to your spouse, "You are more important than what I have used to distract and soothe myself." The greatest blessing you can offer your spouse is your full-bodied attention and delight.

- What are some areas that need you to take this kind of "hell, no" action to prioritize and protect your marriage?
- What steps might you take to follow through to bless your spouse?

Heaven, Yes

We are meant to create goodness together. Putting your foot on the neck of evil is one thing—it touches our deep desire to see evil pay. But we are meant for more, which involves creating beauty for God's glory. We create beauty every time we move to bring the Lord's prayer into action: ". . . on earth as it is in heaven" (Matthew 6:10). Similar to the unique, personalized words of blessing, you and your spouse work together to create goodness. This might include the following:

- Picking up trash in your neighborhood and planting flowers along the road
- Growing vegetables to give away rather than sell at the farmers market
- Baking fabulously thick and gooey chocolate chip cookies for your family
- Starting a 509 plan for your grandchildren
- Looking at the young man busing your table and telling him he is doing a great job and asking if you can speak to his supervisor to sing his praises
- Vacuuming your spouse's ridiculously dirty car without making a snide comment
- Heading out on a hike with a new app to study flowers together
- Taking a lesson together on how to stretch and breathe for greater health
- Going to your spouse's yoga class even if you feel ridiculous

The list is endless. The key is cocreated, imaginative play that brings you both the opportunity to risk some degree of failure. Sitting on the couch, watching a movie, eating popcorn, talking a little, and then going to bed is fine. But if that is your primary way of saying "heaven, yes," then your heaven is barely outside the antechamber of hell.

If you are trying to implement change at this juncture in your marriage, then "heaven, yes" activities provide fresh opportunities for shared experiences that draw you closer. Again, it doesn't particularly matter what you do—it's doing whatever it is together. Whether you bake banana bread, run a marathon, or start a ministry, all goodness grows God's glory.

- What do you both enjoy doing that brings goodness to yourselves and others?
- What do you love to do that brings more beauty to the world?
- How can your spouse join you in what you love?
- What things can you do to join your spouse in what he or she loves?

6 . 2

How Can You Both Thrive in Your Marriage?

Courageously facing hard realities . . . with your spouse will not only deepen your intimacy but also strengthen you, move you closer to God's heart, and make room for more joy. It isn't a question of whether you'll suffer, but whether you'll suffer together and with the Spirit.

THE DEEP-ROOTED MARRIAGE, P. 178

By this point you have risked, strained, suffered, and remained in the process long enough to begin experiencing the fruits of a deep-rooted marriage. The challenge now becomes how to sustain the growth you're experiencing in order to continue producing good fruit. Two key practices can help you in this endeavor: pruning envy and relational opposition and cultivating relationships with other allies.

In the seen and unseen realm, a good marriage is a danger to complacency and despair. It may seem hyperbolic—and indeed, it is tragic—but few marriages develop deep, abiding roots. Most "good" marriages don't engage what is required to grow. The vast majority achieve a degree of pleasure and ease and seldom move beyond relative comfort. If you choose a different path related to what we have asked you to attend and engage in, your marriage will grow and be noticeable to others.

It would be delightful if what is noticed draws others to desire what you have experienced. In a few cases, it will. In many cases, it won't. For those who see and don't change, the most typical response will be envy. It is like seeing someone win the lottery. We all imagine what it would be like to gain a sudden windfall and envy those who do. What is not addressed, however, is that your growing joy is not a windfall but the product of walking through the valley of the shadow of death.

Envy is a lust to consume what others have while also wanting to ruin what you enjoy. Most desire the fruit without the labor. It is almost impossible for most people and couples to accept that someone envies you. Knowing how to undermine envy and relational opposition is crucial if you are to thrive individually and jointly.

The other vital element that can help you sustain growth is relationship and community with other similarly focused allies. Giving to others what has been given to you multiplies the blessings for all. In the process, you and your spouse also exercise your gifts and talents as a team, stimulating your creativity while enriching your connection.

- Who are some couples whose marriages you have admired or even envied? What do they have together that you want to emulate or experience with your spouse?
- Beyond your spouse, who are the people presently helping, supporting, and encouraging your marriage to thrive? What do you need from these allies moving forward?

Breaking the Surface

The energy of envy from others is sometimes subtle and complicated—and easy to miss. But it is felt and often compromises friendships and familial relationships. For example, consider how you respond to an invitation. A decision needs to be made regarding plans with other couples, and your spouse says, "We'd love to be part of the plan, but before we commit, we will need to spend some time as a couple talking about it before we say yes."

What? You mean one of you won't accept an invitation without consulting the other? And what needs to be addressed and discussed? Don't you both want to go? If you say to your friend or family member extending the invitation, "We never decide without time to pray, ponder, and think it through together. Our relationship is more important than the decision," then you have defied the natural order of how people typically respond to invitations. When you make decisions jointly, respecting input from your spouse as well as yourself, then the result will be, to some degree, shock and pushback. In other words, expect envy.

Consider another example. A conflict occurs between you and your spouse in the presence of others. The one who feels hurt says, "I don't like where this conversation is moving. We have worked on it before, and it seems to be happening here and now." This public statement is bold and might convey anger and contempt if motivated by old default defenses, which others might find uncomfortable as well as secretly satisfying. If offered with honesty and kindness, however, it is startling to others.

If your spouse, then, were to say, "Oh, no. You're right. I'm using humor to keep myself from feeling vulnerable. I am so sorry. Let me try again," then people would freak out. Rarely does this happen in real space and time. We all see one another's failures and either ignore them or talk about them in private. To have the ability to self-adjust and redirect for the sake of goodness and honor is stunning. The result will be shock and awe, followed by envy. Yes, you will be talked about, and it will be with something other than amazement. The capacity to grow together in public commands others' attention.

Perhaps you and your spouse engage in a conversation with another friend or couple in which you talk honestly about the effects of your past on the way you each relate to one another when there is failure. You then share how kindness and curiosity have replaced old patterns to bring you closer. You are not boasting or patronizing others with your wisdom—you are simply telling the truth about your hard-earned and grace-filled gratitude. You are telling the truth about your failures—past and present—and telling the truth about the power of the resurrection in the here and now. You are storytelling and inviting others to the intersection of death and life.

What impact would such a conversation have? As you grow together as a couple, you will naturally want to invite others to desire more. Your intentions are for good, yet others may not want to receive what you intend as a gift of vulnerability and hopefulness. Desire for goodness can be dangerous and often must be defended against envy. So don't be surprised by dismissiveness, superficial compliments, or a direct critical attack. Regardless of the response of others, continue to focus on what you and your spouse need and desire to keep your connection growing.

- Where, when, how, and from whom have you encountered direct and more subtle envy?
- How would you likely have responded or been triggered by the envy of others in the past?
- When have you tended to manage others' envy by denying their harm or explaining it away?

- How can you undermine their envy without directly addressing it or undercutting yourself?
- What's required for you and your spouse to remain united when others envy or attack the new growth and goodness you reveal to them?

Letting In the Light

A simple principle to life is that what we are given is meant to be given away. All gifts are meant for a season until they mature us and run their course, and then they are meant to be given as gifts to someone else. This is true of money, of physical objects, and even more so with the gifts of God.

You have worked hard, perhaps harder than anything else you have done in life. You have received beyond the due labor of your hard work and experienced the gift of love that comes not as the result of hard work and earned favor but as a gift of God. For example, consider how you have chosen not to resort to contempt when something in the present activates feelings and bodily memories from the past. Instead, you have committed to extending kindness, well aware that your kindness relies less on willpower and more on the gift of God's grace that you receive and offer to yourself and your spouse.

Keep a gift beyond its time, and it not only ages but perishes. Give it away and the gift given enriches the giver even more than the original gift offered. But the risk of giving what you have learned through this process may seem too big and overwhelming. Nonetheless, consider the outrageous possibility of offering what only you and your spouse can offer to other couples by starting a marriage group. Ask a few couples if they want to read through and engage with *The Deep-Rooted Marriage* book and this companion guidebook as a structured catalyst for group discussion.

You might respond with, "What? Are you crazy? This process has been so disruptive for us—we're still processing right now and will be for some time! How, in the name of God, could I ask other couples to join us?"

Indeed, what a wise petition: "in the name of God." And yes, you need to be a bit off your rocker to invite others to meander through the dark valleys of trauma, abuse, failure, and the hope of redemption. But what else will you do with your marriage and the work of God but give it away?

How to begin? Here are some progressive suggestions:

- Talk about what you are learning with friends who might be interested.
- Mention the book. Gift a couple with a copy and see whether they are interested in talking about what they are learning and hearing your thoughts and experiences after engaging in it.
- If there is any resonance and interest, talk about your desire to meet with couples to grow together as you invite one another to honesty and humility.
- Start the group for a limited period so no one feels bound to an endless process. Start with the assessment section and the origin story. Open the door to trauma and triggers and talk about what you are finding helpful to disrupt the past and create a new present.
- Follow the Spirit as to what needs to be addressed in each couple's marriage and personal life. Give generously and lovingly but remember that you're not responsible for changing others. Trust the Spirit to do what only God can do through the power of his love.

Living Water

You began this process of growing deeper roots in your marriage by assessing where you were and how you had arrived at that place. As you look forward together and consider how to sustain your growth and produce good fruit, it's essential to assess where you are and where you're going. Your relationship is far from perfect, yet you are growing closer and experiencing new levels of intimacy as you remain attuned to one another. In order to thrive together, consider what's ahead, where you're headed next, and what supplies and resources are needed to get there.

We, Dan and Steve, begin by identifying and reflecting on our current seasons of life. Steve and Lisa are in the five-year period of major marital adjustment that comes with the empty nest. It is not a single year, as some presume, but a major period of beginning again, testing, experimenting, failing, and reconfiguring what lies ahead in one's marriage journey. Most couples fail to use this period for major renovation and restoration.

Dan and Becky are in their seventies and entering life's final seasons. We are no longer young and able to make plans with confidence and ease as we have seen what disruption, disease, and death have brought to many of our friends. We can't escape the inevitability that one of us will precede the other, nor can we dwell on the inevitable to ruin what remains. It is a period that sends many couples fleeing to bucket lists, travel, and heightened distractions. Most couples fail to use this period for major reflection and wisdom.

What season of life are you in? Maybe you are married with no children but carrying a heavy load at your job. Maybe you're juggling your careers along with parenting or caring for your own aging parents. Or perhaps you're an empty nester trying to find a new rhythm or entering retirement.

Each season is fraught with its own demands and dangers. To a degree, each requires a new marriage negotiation and a return to address all that we have invited you to consider. If you begin at an earlier season, the process will be difficult but easier than for those who begin later in life. However, no one and no marriage, no matter how old and infirm, can say it is too late. The old cliché that old dogs can't learn new tricks is a lie. The truth is nothing is impossible. With God's help, old dogs can enjoy new tricks.

As you think through where you are and where you're going, consider the timeless wisdom offered by the author of Ecclesiastes:

> There is a time for everything,
>> and a season for every activity under the heavens:
>> a time to be born and a time to die,
>> a time to plant and a time to uproot,
>> a time to kill and a time to heal,
>> a time to tear down and a time to build,
>> a time to weep and a time to laugh,
>> a time to mourn and a time to dance,
>> a time to scatter stones and a time to gather them,
>> a time to embrace and a time to refrain from embracing,
>> a time to search and a time to give up,
>> a time to keep and a time to throw away,
>> a time to tear and a time to mend,
>> a time to be silent and a time to speak,
>> a time to love and a time to hate,
>> a time for war and a time for peace.

ECCLESIASTES 3:1–8

- What season of life are you in? How would you describe your current season with your spouse?
- What are the demands, dangers, rewards, and responsibilities of your current season? Which ones concern you the most? Why?
- What are you enjoying about where you are at this point in your life? What challenges come with this season?
- What's the next season ahead of you? How can you and your spouse prepare now for what you want to experience then?
- How do you want to experience your marriage on your next milestone anniversary? Whether it's your fifth or tenth, your twenty-fifth or fiftieth, how can you and your beloved move in the same direction, united and not merely parallel?

Sharing Fruit

As you begin where you are, which we hope is not where you were when you started this guidebook, you can enjoy the present growth and good fruit while being mindful of what's ahead. Just as a wise farmer or vintner focuses on what's required to maximize the current harvest, he or she also maintains an awareness of the next season as well as the next cycle of seasons required for the coming harvest. As you consider where you are and what's ahead, three primary questions can provide illumination: What does transition from this season to the next look like? What challenges can we anticipate facing in this transition? What do we need to transition well into the next season?

You identified and described your present season in the previous section. Look back at what you wrote and consider whether there's anything you want to add about where you are right now. Now, consider what you recognize as your next major season. Are you moving from the early years of marriage into an expanded family? Or focusing on educational and career goals for one or both of you? Moving from parenting adolescents into becoming empty nesters? Try to be as objective as possible in noting your next big transition.

This consideration invites you to name the contours of the terrain you are traveling—and what lies around the bend ahead. It may seem obvious—you are empty nesters or you are newlyweds. But the terrain must be engaged far more than the label. What realities do you need to address regarding where you live, how much time you need to spend at work or developing skills to advance in your profession, the implications for friendships, free time, finances, sex, time away from home, family, pets, vacations, and so much more? Use the questions below to create a blueprint for bridging your current season into the next.

- Create a list of five to ten activities that make up your normal week during this season of life.
- Take each activity and imagine how it will change as you consider what is ahead. What will remain the same? What might you relinquish in order to create space for what the next season holds?
- What will be the gain in the coming new era? What will be the loss?

Speculating about the challenges ahead requires faith. Such anticipation is necessary for preparation and prevention, yet inevitably, some unexpected obstacles will leave you reeling. Nonetheless, you maintain the present tension of what you can predict and expect with the uncertainty of the future.

We love to change when it is our choice. Most of us are less excited about having to change because it is required. But mental and emotional preparation can go a long way in allowing you to move into the future step-by-step. Imagine what your life will look like in the next season. Consider what will be required as you enter your new era.

- What will be the new challenges of what you will gain and lose in the new era?
- What themes from your past will resurface because of what is ahead?
- What is required now for you as a person and a couple to enter the new era?

Finally, consider who you want to become moving forward—which in turn overlaps with the kind of marriage you want to grow into. Such consideration might seem insipidly obvious at first. You think, *I want to become a better person. I want to grow a better marriage, be a more loving and attuned partner to my spouse.* True, but the end goal and process will be tedious and pointless if you remain abstract. You will change to the degree that you follow your deepest heart desires with particularity and passion. Whom do you really want to become? Your answer begins by addressing these questions:

- Consider asking Jesus, "What parts of me are you wanting to redeem at this point?" What do you hear?
- How much curiosity and kindness do you have toward the parts that God desires to grow?
- How can you consider praying with your spouse about this "becoming," and how can your engagement about these changes flourish in the face of mounting challenges?

Each season of life requires us to let go of what has enabled us to do well in the preceding season and take on new wisdom, skills, and equipment to move into the next season. As an example, I (Dan) need to wear my hearing aids all the time. I don't. If I know I am alone and reading or writing, I refuse to poke these annoying megaphones in my ear canals. But I don't know when Becky is going to ask a question or want to talk. This requires me to keep the hearing aids near and put them in even if the conversation lasts a minute. Irritating. But required.

While you cannot predict with full accuracy the changes, challenges, and needs of the future, you can still anticipate what adjustments and resources will be needed to flourish together in the next season.

- What will be the biggest adjustment you will make as a couple in the next season? How are you preparing for it now?
- What sacrifices will you each need to make in order to sustain the level of intimacy you desire in your marriage in this next season?
- What are some of the supplies and resources presently lacking that you will need as you move into the next season of life? What will you need to leave behind?

6 . 3

Nourishing the Roots

Play is crucial to intimacy. When we aren't intentional about incorporating it into our life together, we rob our marriages of the nutrients they need. While a relationship might go on surviving without play, it will not flourish.

THE DEEP-ROOTED MARRIAGE, P. 185

Congratulations! You have reached the final section of this guidebook. This means you have done considerable and life-changing work on yourself as well as your marriage. As you complete these Nourishing the Roots exercises one last time, celebrate the fact that progress has been made and growth has occurred. You may not see it or feel it or believe it will last, but that does not invalidate the realities, visible and invisible, that God is at work and change is occurring—within you and your spouse.

One of the best ways to celebrate new growth as well as to sustain it is to play together. Play is perhaps the most overlooked and underutilized practice for a healthy life and a vibrant marriage. Undeniably, play is essential for growth. Without it, we simply can't flourish and keep growing.

So the focus for this final joint exercise is a special experience of play, one that requires each of you simply to enjoy delighting in the other's company. After your time of play together, you can then reflect on how to continue incorporating play in your marriage. Finally, you can spend some time reflecting together on the joint progress made over the course of completing this guidebook.

Playtime

Play is meant to cultivate delight. Children at a playground will call to their parents, "Watch!" They long for their parents to see and delight in them. We have that same longing in us as adults, and there is a purity to it. Watching communicates desire and invitation—both for our joy of being watched and for the joy of the other who watches us.

Deep roots require the nourishment that only play can provide. The soil of your heart is impenetrable unless you tend to it with intentional play. That is what will slowly help you establish deep roots over time and bring forth fruit.

Playing together strengthens your friendship with your spouse, and research shows that marriages built on friendship experience more contentment than those that are not. Play cultivates intimacy, which, as we've said, means "to make known." We make ourselves known in play. It fosters emotional connection as we send the message "I want to be with you. You matter, and we matter." Play delights in what might seem trivial or nonessential, creating space for frivolity, laughter, and good old-fashioned fun.

Enjoying play together also increases your sense of safety as you reassure your spouse that you want to stay close, that you enjoy simply being together and doing something that doesn't have to be productive together. Through play, your actions say, "I choose you, and I choose us."

Play also releases chemical responses in your body—oxytocin (which helps regulate emotions) and dopamine (which is associated with pleasure). This is no surprise. There is pleasure when you play!

Playing together in your marriage helps each of you to feel known and loved. It provides the restorative reassurance that you are not alone. And as you continue the rituals and stay in the rhythms of them, play makes your bond stronger. It softens tensions and eases repair in conflict. It attunes and lightens burdens. It laughs at inside jokes. It helps close distance and even heals hurts. It tells us: "We are on the same team. We are for each other. We are choosing each other."

Integrating more play into your relationship will require intentionality and might feel like a disruption at first. That is to be expected with anything new. Choose to prioritize it because you want to choose closeness with your partner. When you do, you'll be embracing a change agent: the intention to bless. In simple ways, you take in the presence of your spouse with wonder, delight, and gratitude. In everyday moments, you'll be saying "heaven, yes" to the beauty you can create together.

So start to consider what you can do together repeatedly. How could you have consistent experiences of connection, even in short windows of time? Play can be adventuresome and physical but need not be elaborate or require exertion. Here are some examples of rhythms and rituals that incorporate play in very accessible, feasible ways:

- Sitting on the porch, watching the sunset
- Doing a few yoga stretches
- Praying for each other
- Having a glass of wine before dinner
- Sharing experiences that you can both laugh about
- Playing a game together
- Completing a puzzle
- Writing a song, poem, skit, or letter together
- Looking at photos together
- Exploring new places (cities, neighborhoods, restaurants, markets) together
- Taking a meandering Sunday drive through a beautiful region

These are just to get you started. Just think about what you both enjoy and keep it simple. Then build your practice so that it becomes a habit you both anticipate and look forward to. Ask yourself, "What are a few ways we can begin to integrate a consistent ritual? What's something that feels doable to start with?"

Remember, it can be incredibly simple, and there's really no agenda. It is about simply being in the presence of each other.

It's a ritual of presence. It communicates, "You matter, and we matter."

It's a ritual of loyalty. It says to your partner, "I choose you."

And it's a ritual of remembering your togetherness: "Let me remind you: I'm here with you. You're not alone, and neither am I. We are together. Let's celebrate!"

- Let one of the items bulleted above inspire you or come up with your own. Then, designate a time and place for you and your spouse to meet for no other purpose than to play. You can play pickleball, pick berries, stroll through the park, plant herbs, create sculptures from Legos, or go to the amusement park. Choose something that will allow you to unplug and devote undivided attention to each other and have fun together.

Keep Playing

After you play, wait a day or two and then reconvene to discuss what you enjoyed most about your time together. Use the following questions and prompts to facilitate your discussion, but feel free to digress and simply enjoy a conversation about how to practice play as a vital part of your relationship.

- Where did you go and what did you do to play together? Why did you choose this context for play?
- What did each of you enjoy most about your experience of play? What made you feel carefree, childlike, and connected?
- Brainstorm a list of ways you would like the two of you to play going forward.
- What's something you enjoyed playing as a child that you could return to now with your spouse? How can you invite your spouse into this aspect of your story?
- Look at your schedules for the coming week and plan your next playdate. Even if it's sipping coffee and watching the sunrise, put it on both your calendars and make it a priority.

Growth Chart

If you have been around children for any length of time, you have likely recorded their growth in some way. It might be taking a photo in the same setting and pose each year on their birthdays. You might have a certain doorway or wall where you measure their height and mark it alongside their age. Whatever it is, the intention is to see and celebrate their growth.

Keeping track of your growth as a couple is worth recognizing and celebrating just as much. Completing this guidebook presents a natural opportunity to assess where you started with the work you've been doing recently as compared to where you see yourselves now. For inspiration, return together to the ebenezer you established back in Part 1.

You'll recall this monument, regardless of size or location, draws on the biblical tradition of marking sacred places as reminders of God's goodness and faithfulness. Whether you gathered a few smooth stones on a bookshelf or erected a special sculpture in your garden, your ebenezer has even more significance now. You are not where you were. You have done hard and painful digging, and now you are tasting the fruit of your labors.

Even if you're still struggling, consider the effort as part of your growing pains. As you both continue working on your own issues lingering from past trauma, celebrate your awareness both in yourself and your spouse. You have invited one another into a deeper level of knowing and growing together.

Finally, to help you articulate these differences, spend some time discussing the changes you have experienced as well as the growth you have seen in your spouse. Consider writing down your thoughts, feelings, and observations in a jointly held journal for your marriage, providing a record you can review and build on at regular intervals. Use the following questions and prompts to help you reflect on and delight in where you are now—and where you are going next.

- What's one area of growth you've experienced over the course of completing this guidebook? How has your growth manifested in your marriage and the ways you interact with your spouse?
- What's one area of growth you've witnessed in your spouse during this same period? How has his or her growth impacted you?
- What triggers have lost their power or no longer result in the old default patterns in each of you? When have you most recently experienced kindness rather than contempt for yourself and for your spouse?
- What's one of your biggest takeaways from the work you've done through this guidebook? What do you know—about yourself, about your spouse, about God—now at a deeper level?
- What three words best describe how you're feeling about the future of your relationship? How can you continue to thrive and celebrate your growth together?

Dig deeper with us in our video series using the below QR code.

A Note from the Authors

We crafted this companion guide to be similar to the experience of good marriage counseling. We are therapists, and we think, for good or ill, like therapists—meaning, we needed a wise, kind, and brilliant collaborator who could take our insights and weave them into a message that was linear and easy to navigate.

Thirty-some years ago, I (Dan) had the privilege of having Dudley Delffs and his remarkable bride, Dotti, go through the counseling program I was part of in Colorado. When Carrie Marrs, our lifesaving editor, suggested Dudley, I was stunned that someone as renowned and skilled as Dudley would be willing to work with us.

Dudley brought depth and beauty along with structure and clarity. This book would not be what it is without his gifts and the goodness of his and Dotti's marriage. We wanted him to have the final words in this offering.

Dan and Steve

———

When Dotti and I studied with Dan decades ago, his insights on relationships, faith, and human and spiritual development shaped how we saw ourselves, each other, and God. Although we've stayed in touch with Dan and Becky, opportunities to work together remained elusive until Carrie Marrs asked me to help with a guidebook for *The Deep-Rooted Marriage*.

This book, written by Dan and my new friend Steve Call, stunned me. I read, write, and edit for a living, but rarely have I been as engaged, captivated, and deeply moved as I have with this content. It benefits from Dan and Steve's years of professional experience but much more from their hard work to become better humans, husbands, fathers, and friends. Their raw honesty and courageous vulnerability reflect the power of God at work in our lives—when we're willing to invite him into the messy process of being known and loved.

Working on this guidebook proved to be more challenging than I expected and more transformative than I dared to hope. So much of myself and my own marriage stared back at me, compelling me to risk loving my wife in more honest, caring ways. Finishing this project coincided with our thirty-fifth wedding anniversary, which inspired me to write a blessing for my wife to give her as part of our celebration. I pray that this guidebook blesses you and your spouse with the same inspiration to uproot old cycles, nourish the love between you, and grow deeper roots.

Dudley

RECONNECT INSTITUTE

*"Story is the context
for how we are known
by our spouse."*

Dr. Steve Call

The Reconnect Institute invites couples to courageously explore relational patterns that disrupt connection in their marriage while offering resources, insights, and tools to grow in greater intimacy. We help you experience more profound levels of awareness and understanding of yourself and one another, leading to a renewed connection in your marriage.

———

Offerings:

- Marriage Story Intensives
- Couples Intensives
- Story Groups

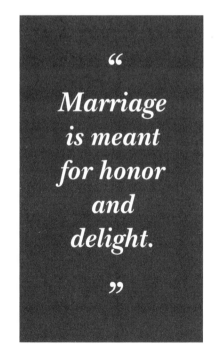

"

*Marriage
is meant
for honor
and
delight.*

"

thereconnectinstitute.com

Dr. Steve and Lisa Call

Allender Center
AT THE SEATTLE SCHOOL

Marriage is a meeting of two profoundly different stories.

We each carry core stories from our past—stories that have shaped us in ways we might not even realize. Stories of disappointment and desire, of hurt and hope. These stories impact how we show up in the present, especially in our closest relationships.

At the Allender Center, we invite you and your spouse to continue to explore your stories together. Through our marriage courses, conferences, and retreats, you can move toward greater understanding, honor, and delight in your relationship.

> "You must understand the *past* if you want to change the *present*."
>
> - Dr. Dan Allender

Start your journey today at:
theallendercenter.org/marriage